WITH GOD ON OUR SIDE

By Anthony Tuttle

ZEBRA BOOKS

KENSINGTON PUBLISHING CORP.

ZEBRA BOOKS

are published by

KENSINGTON PUBLISHING CORP.
521 Fifth Avenue
New York, N. Y. 10017.

Copyright © 1978 by Anthony Tuttle

All rights reserved. No part of this book may be reproduced in any form or by any means without the prior written consent of the Publisher, except brief quotes used in reviews.

First Printing: February, 1978

Printed in the United States of America

In their own words, from their own hearts...

"I had packed my bags again. I was running away from the rehab center. But I heard a voice saying, 'go back, go back.' It wasn't a stupendous thing, like Paul on the road to Damascus, but for me it was dramatic because, in all that confusion, God had time for me. Just those simple words. 'Go back, go back.'"

"I'm trapped, I said, and, all right, God, you've brought me here. I could not climb up to get out. I came up one side and down the other; I couldn't get past the waterfall. I thought I was going to die and I cried out to God. Suddenly, on the rim of the opposite cliff, was a man. He yelled to me, 'Can you get out?' 'No,' I hollered. And he started down the cliff. Halfway down, he fell. His arm was bleeding, but he got to his feet and kept on going. He said, 'All right, hold my hand. Follow me. Step by step.'

"Later, I came to understand that that day at the waterfall God had revealed something of His son to me through the man who came down from the cliff, bleeding, who said, 'Follow me. Step by step.'"

"I heard the Lord call me by name. I knew it was Jesus talking. He said I'd come to a crossroads in my life and not to be confused or afraid. That he was my good shepherd, that he was going to save me. As He spoke to me, I felt the warmth of His love flowing into me. And, suddenly, I was born again."

...Here are stories of people just like you who have battled emptiness, despair and confusion—and then were Born Again

WITH GOD ON OUR SIDE

*This book is dedicated
to all those people
who made it possible,
especially
Joe and Lou and Paul.*

*Reach beyond the reach of your hand
and the stars will meet you halfway.*

— Anchanu, the Prophet

Preface

Like a flame that gives a candle its meaning and purpose, so does each decade seem lit by particular events and phenomena that give it its definition and historical importance. The 1940s—World War II and the beginning of the Cold War. The 1950s—the McCarthy Era, the Silent Generation, the Beat Generation, Ike's fatherly concern.

And the 60s? The answers are almost too obvious. The Kennedy assassination. The Vietnam War. The Beatles. More assassination—Robert Kennedy and Martin Luther King. Student protest. A nation at war abroad and with itself.

The decade isn't over yet, but what of the 1970s? Of course, Watergate. The end of the Vietnam War. And Richard Nixon's resignation. And the settling effect Gerald Ford tried to bring to the country after such traumatic times, war and riot and a government led by deceitful, paltry men.

And then Jimmy Carter. He promised to bring us back to ourselves, back to our essential goodness, he said, and, yes, he said, he was Born Again. He was a Born Again Christian.

In any summation of the notable events or phenomena of the 1970s, high in priority would be the emergence of a return to "old time religion." Country and western singers professed it and sang about it. Famous athletes avowed it. Charles Colson, one of Nixon's closest advisors, wrote about his sudden acceptance of Jesus, and if at first one was skeptical, if one thought it was a kind of public apology for past sins, all one had to do was read his book. One knew he meant business, that his conversion was real.

The procession of celebrities who announced they had turned to God often cast suspicion on the validity of their faith. There seemed to be a sudden bandwagon abroad in the land, and there were a lot of footprints left on the ground. Yet millions of simpler folk were also climbing on; it wasn't just Roy Clark or Pat Boone, Charles Colson or Tom Phillips, the president of Raytheon.

New congregations arose out of the spirit of a country that longed to be healed. Old congregations welcomed new members. And in some communities, such as Darien, Connecticut, the born again movement both revitalized and divided local churches. St. Paul's Episcopal Church, headed by Father Fullam, increased its membership sixfold with a charismatic service. But some old guard members were scornful of the frenzied, emotional nature of the new Church. They deemed it "fast-food religion" and now a "McDonald's of a church."

Hopefully, the testimony contained in these pages explains the Born Again experience and, more importantly, reveals the emotional path traveled from emptiness and despair towards hope and passion, from darkness to light. Whether the goal attained be bogus and the journey misdirected, only the reader can decide. The words are the speaker's only proof, the tools of his faith, and the echoes between them. So let the listener decide. He may himself be suddenly moved to the Lord or to a deeper understanding of the born again experience or he may simply say, "Is this guy serious?"

No matter one's conviction, I think a common denominator links all the stories herein, whether they be ones that lead to an acceptance of Jesus or a freedom from drugs or alcohol. In each testimony from the remarkable people you are about to meet, the will to search, to question, to doubt and to not doubt always takes precedence over despair, over resignation. And it is this mesh of striving, like separate hands joined, that at first shows us the wonder and beauty of their humanness and then, if it be so, their ascension to God.

Anthony Tuttle
New York City
November 10, 1977

CARL is thirty-five. A thoughtful, gentle man, he is an accomplished composer of devotional songs.

I was raised Jewish. And when I was young, I would hear God's name taken in vain and I was sure He would strike us down.

My parents didn't know the Lord; I don't blame them, so I grew up with a very vague understanding of who God was and at a certain point, I saw that the world was mad, therefore, I decided I might as well be crazy too. So I made God an image of my own madness. I had a choice, either I viewed life as very funny. Or very unjust. I chose to view it as very funny.

My premise was that there was nothing serious, so I tried to live that way. In school, I fit everything into my particular pattern of manic behavior. If the teacher said, pull down the shades, Carl, I ripped them down. I was always the prankster, I was always the one who "did" it. This kept up until the eleventh grade and then I realized that I would never get into college if I continued to play the fool. There were even times when I was on probation. So whatever I did, I also encouraged others to do.

This was Camden High, in New Jersey, and my brother had gone there before me. He was a brilliant student, so I left a lot of heads shaking wondering what had happened, gene-wise. But I had a great deal of fun, being the clown. It carried over for many years. It was like trying to live like the Marx Brothers. I wrote for my high school paper and got an assignment to interview the Three Stooges. Their relationship to the material world was exactly where I was at. They were very old at this point, not very manic, but I went to interview them at the Latin Casino in Philadelphia, and I had never been happier.

I was seventeen by then and very underdeveloped both mentally and emotionally. I thought of school as a training ground for comedy. I wasn't malicious. I was just very rebellious.

After high school, I went to college for a year but I did very poorly. It was a strange experience. I hardly spoke to anyone. I took journalism, and there was a requirement that you had to do thirty hours live on the college radio station. I never did one minute because I was too petrified. I was afraid of confronting people. I lived at home, I had no social life, I didn't go out with girls. I didn't drive a car, I had no desire to do any of those things. I just wanted to eat. I was very overweight in those days.

I lasted only a year in college and after that I decided that I wanted to go to acting school—even though I had never been in a play. I had studied singing, had even sung at a nightclub for three weeks, until my voice changed. It changed right in the middle of a song—and I got fired on New Year's Eve.

For me, studying acting meant living in New York City. I had no money but I decided this was what I had to do. I remember the day I left. My mother was at the door. She gave me fifty dollars and said, "We'll give you a week to make good."

From 1961 through 1963, they paid for the entire tuition at the acting school, the Neighborhood Playhouse. It was a very difficult experience because, for the first time in my life, I had to take myself seriously. It was very painful. The whole structure was based on self-discovery—and I thank God for it. It brought me out of myself. In front of other people, it showed me what I was.

I was invited back the second year and did even better. But I remember the teacher saying, "Do you really want to act? You don't seem to want to do this."

After I graduated, I did some summer stock, then came back to the city but I couldn't get any acting work. I just didn't have the desire to break down doors. So I started writing comedy. If this is the way I see the world, I thought, perhaps there's a living in it. I lived in a hotel room, and I never went outside. The owner asked me if I wanted a job in the lobby. I would call the comedians I knew through a comedy workshop and they liked the material, but they ripped me off. They would never pay me. I learned a new word—"spec." I lived on "spec."

Finally, I realized that this life had no substance. I left New York and went back to New Jersey and worked for Campbell Soup for a year—until I could get enough money and go right back to New York. When I did, I met a piano player, who was just as manic as I was, and could take nothing seriously. We wanted to develop a singing act but neither one of us could finish a song, so a comedy act developed. We took it to the Improvisation, a club for young comics, and started trying it out. Someone saw us and got us an interview for the *Merv Griffin Show*. I had been a "comedian" for just a month and, suddenly, it's the big time. I was terrified. At the interview, I was totally manic. But the producer liked it. "All right," he said, "we'll put you on."

I was totally panicked. I did the show and was absolutely goofy on it. Poor Merv Griffin had no idea what I was doing. Afterwards, he said, "What was that?" I don't know if the audience was laughing at me or with me. All I know is I was glad that it was over.

We started working regularly at different clubs in New York, and up the Borscht Belt in the Catskills, but I had no heart for it. It was just a working out some kind of extreme anxiety. I even included God in my act. As a king of mockery. There was a sketch about going to heaven and what you'd find when you got there. Achilles would have a shoe store. That sort of thing. That was my notion of God.

We did the act for three years. I had started smoking a lot of dope and I saw that my moral judgment was slipping. To make additional money, I began to do porno movies and pose for porno magazines. I did them because I didn't think anything of it. But once, I went into a store and opened up a magazine and there I was. Actually seeing myself brought home what I was doing. I knew it was all coming back to me. I was sowing some terrible seeds.

I needed a change of scene; I knew that. So I quit the world of comedy and went to California. I got a part in a movie but my performance was awful, and I couldn't grasp that. I was devastated. So I quit performing and started writing a movie. It was called *Impediments,* about a comedian who is always looked on as funny but no longer had a need to be funny yet was forced to be funny. It took me two years to finish and I thought it was good.

At first, on the coast, I lived in Hollywood and I did a lot of walking. I didn't know how to drive. Then I moved to Venice, by the ocean, and I was stoned a great deal of the time. I was also very involved in the occult. In palmistry. Astrology. In fruit diets. I was beginning to search.

The fruit diet made me very sick and very spacy. My entire day consisted to going to the health food store and squeezing peaches. I would go four times a day. I lived that way for about six months. That was all I looked forward to, this mucusless diet, trying to get all the mucus out of my system so I could live forever in perfection. But I was also looking for God.

It happened early one morning. I had been thinking about camping out, it had been on my mind for weeks. But I was afraid. I had never camped out at all. One night, early into the morning, I heard a voice and the voice said, "Go into the desert and thank God for your life."

It wasn't a voice from my head. It was in my heart. I said, this must be God. It was a very clear voice and very firm, so I borrowed a friend's sleeping bag and I took a suitcase with me. I asked Him, where should I go? He said, "Why don't you go to Palm Springs? To the waterfall there." I took a bus and got off at the right stop and made a right turn toward the canyon. But it was Easter time and priests were there and the authorities wouldn't let anyone else in. I said, okay, I don't want to cause trouble, so I'll find another place.

I hitched a ride and got off on the highway and walked right off into the desert, clutching my snake bite kit. I felt wonderful. I thanked God for my existence. I thanked Him for the wide open sky. I stayed there for about an hour, but there were snake holes in the ground so I said, if I stay here, I'll probably die. This is crazy. At that point, I began to doubt that it was God that I had heard. I said, I must have been really stoned, so I'll go home now.

I hitched a ride back to the bus stop and the man who picked me up asked, "Where are you going?" I told him I'd wanted to go to the waterfall but I couldn't get in. He said, "I'll get you in." And he did. That night I camped out at the foot of the canyon and I thanked God all night. That sky was amazing. All night I saw stars falling.

The next day I headed for the waterfall. I saw a

cliff that seemed like a short cut, and I started to climb it though it was very treacherous for me. I got halfway up and, suddenly, knew I couldn't go back, so I kept going and went up and over the cliff and down to the waterfall. I stayed for hours. I took out all the beer cans and the garbage people had tossed in the water and had a tremendous time, thanking God, until I realized that I really couldn't get out, that I could not in any way climb up the side of the cliff I'd come down.

I was trapped, so I wrote three letters, explaining who I was and if my body was found, this was why I had come and this was who I was. I didn't know how I would mail the letters.

I stayed there and started to face some big issues in my life. I'm trapped, I said, and, all right, God, you've brought me here. I could not climb up to get out. I came up one side and down the other; now I could either go up that way or cross the waterfall and go up the other way. It looked too treacherous to me. I thought I was going to die and I cried out to God.

Suddenly, on the rim of the opposite cliff, a man appeared, and yelled to me, "Can you get out?" I hollered out "No," and he said, "All right. I'll be right there!" He started down the cliff and when he was halfway down, he fell. His arm was bleeding but he got to his feet and came down to the stream and said, "All right, hold my hand. Follow me, step by step, and watch for loose stones."

I knew I had to trust this man. He held onto me but I kept stepping on the loose rock. Never before had I been so confronted with my own weakness.

But he just kept holding my hand and pulling me up. Without him, I would have fallen. I would have died. I don't know how long it took to lead me out but when we got to the rim I was almost too embarrassed to thank him. He was so calm, so grave. "Have a good time," he said and then was gone.

When I got home, I didn't tell anyone what had happened except that it was something very profound. But I knew that God had done something to me. He had almost taken my life. But he had also saved me. I started thanking God every day and, in thanking Him, I found I was also thanking Jesus. Something had happened in my heart. My intellect had no link to this perception because, being Jewish, I was in a new, mysterious land.

The feeling was euphoric but unsettling, because I had never had a feeling like this, knowing that God had started to deal with my life. Quickly, I got very ill from the fruit diet and had to go to live at a friend's house in Hollywood. He took care of me, and during this time, I came to understand that I had had an actual confrontation with Jesus without ever having read the Bible, that that day at the falls God had revealed something of His son to me through the man who came down from the cliff, bleeding, who said, "Follow me. Step by step."

I came back to New York but sin had still not been dealt with in my life. I knew that something wonderful had happened to me, but I was still smoking too much dope. I finally told my girl I think that Jesus is the answer for my life. Maybe you'd like to be part of that—and that ended that relationship. The occult was also still in my life—darkness and light. I was still into astrology and palmistry. There were many spirits lurking in my life that were not of God, but I still didn't know it. There was power there, but it wasn't yet from God. Thus, I had these two conflicting forces alive in my life. I was walking around the streets with my hands raised in praise, feeling this wonderful experience, but not understanding any of it.

One day, I decided to go into a church. I don't think I had ever been in a church before. It was a Lutheran church on Lexington Avenue and I wanted the pastor to explain what had happened to me. I thought that maybe he could help me. I was very excited, very manic. He thought that I was on LSD and tried to talk me out of Christianity. "You better be sure of this," he said. "You're Jewish and how do I know you're not on acid? How do I know?" I started to doubt myself. Maybe I am crazy, I told myself.

He'd advised me to come back on Sunday for a full-fledged service. So I did. And, for me, it was a very dead experience. It was like a synagogue. The only thing I enjoyed was looking at the windows.

Yet I knew I loved Jesus. I couldn't understand what had happened to me. But I knew that Jesus was God. What that would mean to me, at that point I did not know. I remember one day I went into one of those quarter peep shows and, when I came home, such a feeling of panic came over me that I felt my spirit was going to leave my body. I had done something that brought such guilt to me that I went outside, found a panhandler and I gave him some money. And I didn't know how to deal with that, trying to make up to God for it. But I felt something inside of me, the awareness of sin, for the first time in my life. Then it happened again when I smoked a joint. I had smoked an awful lot of grass and I'd never felt guilty about it. But this time, I had that experience again; I felt my spirit withdrawing from my body, a terrible coldness came over my heart. I said, All right, I'll never smoke grass again. And I'll never go to those peep shows again. So, somehow, God was working repentence into my life.

I had a new girlfriend, a Christian who had backslipped, and she was living with a friend of mine. She told me about a fellowship group and I decided to go to a meeting. I had always had a difficult time relating to Christians. These were the people I'd avoided all my life, people I felt had denied me the life I'd always wanted. I went to the meeting with a lot of craziness in me, still quite manic. I tried to read one of the people's hands there; I talked too much. Yet I knew I loved Jesus and they were kind to me. Even though I saw myself as a little weird, they didn't put me down. The group was called One Flock.

But I didn't go back for months. It didn't feed the pride in me, duplicate that first experience with the Lord which had puffed me up so wondrously. As a matter of fact, that first experience, I think, retarded my spiritual growth for a long while. No one could tell me anything.

Finally, someone told me about a Jewish-Christian temple on West 72nd Street, and I started to go there. For the first time in my life, I heard the Bible and I met other Jews who had experienced Christ, and I felt that I wasn't alone. It was still a difficult time for me because I come from a manic background. For me, there had to be an extreme emotional response to everything. But God was working something much deeper in my life. The Word. His wisdom. Finally, I went back to One Flock and eventually was baptized in The Holy Spirit and began to learn and understand The Word. At One Flock, you could get up and dance before God, you could get up and sing. But if you didn't want to, you didn't have to. At first, I felt inhibited because I didn't want to seem too extreme. But once I began to praise the Lord, sometimes I would go overboard. People would tell me to quiet down, or I would then be too inhibited and need to be stirred up. But I would hear God talking to me, the same voice that told me to go to the desert, and it was a wonderful thing. It took me a long time to learn—but I finally did. There are only three voices you can hear: God's; your own; and the enemy's.

When I came back from California to New York, I had no job and no money. I borrowed a dollar a day to live on and I borrowed my rent and I lived from day to day, thanks to my friends. I lost my phone and I almost lost my apartment on West 46th Street. I borrowed from everyone and I was confessing Jesus to a lot of people. I would go out on the streets and try to convince them. My friend, who lived downstairs, came to the Lord. It was wonderful to see that. But at that point, I was looking for a job every day, never found anything and felt wonderful. One night, a friend and I split a sweet potato.

In December of 1972, I found the job I have now. Being a doorman. Joining the union and having the responsibility of a "straight" job taught me a lot. I learned a great deal from it. Running an elevator, being responsible for people, serving people, mopping the floors was a very humbling experience. At first, I worked just as a porter and had just a wonderful time. I knew this was grace because I could have never done that; my pride wouldn't have let me do "lowly" things like that.

About a year after I came to the Lord, a gift came to me. The Lord told me to play the piano. I was reading a scripture and said to myself, boy, how beautiful! Someone should put that to music. It was the Song of Solomon. So I sat down at a piano but there was a hitch. I didn't know how to play the piano. But when I touched the keys, suddenly music came and the right chords and I wrote my first song. Soon, more and more music came and more personal experience with God, and I started to see how God was going to use me. At that point I was satisfied to be a porter because I was so happy that I knew God. I said to myself, all my life I've looked for the truth, so what does it matter what I do now? I know my place in the universe. I know where I'm going. I know where I belong. All that matters is to live.

So this gift came and I started to play the piano and sing and I feel that this is what God wants me to do. I still can't read music; I have a friend who writes the music down. Will I ever perform? That's the Lord's decision. They're His gifts. If He asks me to perform, I will.

So much has changed.

The biggest change is to be able to see everything from a different set of eyes, from a different heart. To see people and reality and life through God's eyes, through His word, which I could never do before. Before, it was always with a selfish motive. Every conversation had a selfish motive, every piece of work, every action.

Shortly after I asked Jesus into my life, I said to myself, well, that's that. Hurray for me. But very quickly, I learned it's a slow process. Just three weeks ago, I faced a difficult situation. I live on a courtyard and one afternoon I looked out at an opposite window and there was a girl and a guy on a bed and they were making love. I knew I had a decision. To look away and shut the blinds. But God said, "Well, if it bothers you, why don't you just turn away. Why do you have to draw the blinds?" I listened to Him but I could not turn away at all. This—after five years of believing in Him, walking with his Word. So I saw that there was so much of my old nature still in my life. Eventually, I did turn away and I repented. But every day after that, I was drawn to that person's window. I didn't want to come home because I knew that the first thing that would happen would be the Devil and my flesh tempting me with the couple on the bed.

But God did something wonderful. One morning I read something in Romans 6 about being dead to sin, about submitting your members unto God and your eyes and your heart. I'd read it many times before but I read it that morning, and I knew that I had a victory. I knew it was a reality to me. That it would be part of my life. And I wasn't drawn to that window at all that day. I came home the next morning and opened the shade and between Friday afternoon and Saturday morning that girl had moved out. The shades were open and there was no furniture. There was nothing.

SIMON is in his mid-thirties. His father was from Nicaragua and Simon spent his early years in New York's Spanish Harlem. He is now Assistant Director of Teen Challenge, a drug rehabilitation center with branches in many cities throughout the country.

As a boy growing up in Spanish Harlem, I did not have the greatest spiritual or physical environment. As I got older, I started blaming things on this environment and on my family. Maybe if I was born and raised in another state, I used to tell myself, I wouldn't be the way I am. But as a boy, the thing to do was to follow everyone else and what everyone else was doing wrong.

In this case, it was to steal. We stole anything we

could. We would go into five and dime stores or candy stores and then we started hitching rides on the back of buses and going downtown and into Macy's and Gimbel's and Bloomingdale's, just to steal nonsense things. Hats you couldn't use. Shirts that didn't fit you. It was the kick of stealing that mattered.

This was when I was eleven or twelve. I remember I had started smoking cigarettes when I was nine. I was even drinking at that age. I kept getting wilder and less obedient to my parents. I was the youngest of six children and had been told that I was a mistake, which did not make me feel very wanted, and communication with my family got worse and worse because my father was always angry because of the things that me and my brothers and sisters were doing. My father was the kind of man who laid down the law. When the law was broken, terrible beatings would follow.

As I got older, I started going to parties and dances and nightclubs. I remember sneaking into a club without identification when I was sixteen. And one time, I borrowed someone's card to get in. It was a big kick to be around all the grown-ups and the drinking and the pot and the cocaine. By the time I was seventeen, I had already been exposed to coke and I was smoking pot. The guy that turned me on to pot was a close friend of mine but that first time, I got so high, so spaced-out, that I was very frightened. It was like I didn't have control of my mind, and I got pale and felt sick. I saw spots in front of my eyes and, then, after a few hours that went away and the laughter came. Two days later,

I smoked some more and the following week, too. Each time, I had to dish out a dollar and, for me, a dollar was hard money.

Because we were in high school, my friend said, "Look, why don't we do this? Why don't we save our lunch money and we'll chip in two-fifty each and we'll buy a five dollar bag of pot for ourselves." So I said, okay, great. When I went to school the next day, I took a few joints with me and I sold one of them for a buck.

The following week, we started dealing in school on a full-time basis. I dealt in my school, he dealt in his, and we were turning over about an ounce a week. We kept this up for two years until, finally, at my school, they found out. And I was asked to leave.

From then on in, it was all downhill. I was filled with a kind of perverse pride. I made it a big deal to be kicked out of school. I had money from dealing and thought I was a big shot on my block. But my dad really laid down the law now. I had to get a job. And then I got a little break. I got a good job out on Long Island in a radar company. It made me feel as though I was part of something. I was doing something during the day and at night we were still selling our pot. And I had started to use cocaine because there was no way I was going to stick a needle in my arm. Often, I'd take my dog up to the roof and I'd see the junkies up there, cooking up the stuff, sticking needles in their arms, see them getting off and see the blood and I'd get sick just thinking about it.

At the parties in those days—1959—the coke

was good. Very good. And I said to myself, I'm never going to get hooked on the needle. Never. Never. Never. But one night, my friend and I were down at our clubhouse—it was our base of business—and there were eight or nine guys there, all of us getting high and having fun. And that night, I'll never forget it because that was the first time I tried heroin. What I did was sniff it. And the same thing happened as when I tried pot for the first time. I took too much and I got very sick from the quinine and began to vomit. Yet through all that, there was a strange sensation in my body, a feeling I'd never known before. The next morning when I woke up, my stomach killing me, I said, I'm not going to do that again. Never. But a few days later, there was this same buddy of mine, my partner again, and he said, "Do you want to do it again? Are you sure? Do you know what you're doing?" I did it again and this time I didn't take as much as I did the first time and it was a lot better. I felt good inside. That's how I started with heroin.

I sniffed it for two years before I stuck a needle in my arm. Both of us would sell a half a pound of pot and then we would spend all the money on heroin. And the more money we made, the more heroin we bought. We were sniffing it every day and the realization we were hooked just hit us one day. We were sitting in Central Park, smoking pot and drinking, and all of a sudden I looked at him. His nose was running, my own nose was running and my whole body felt sick, and I said, "You know, we're hooked." And we stayed there for a while with the other guys and then we left and bought some more junk.

Soon, things weren't going too well with our pot connection. The money wasn't coming in like it used to. We both knew that it's much easier to sell junk than it is to sell pot, the turnover is a lot faster. But we limited it to pot and started owing the pot guy money. He began to get uptight about this. What was going on? Such good customers all these years. He had never gotten busted. He was very careful. All he sold was pot. It was a perfect connection for us. But it got to the point where one morning I woke up and saw my friend and we counted our money and found we were short. We had no money to buy pot. We had no money to make money. We weren't used to hustling in the streets, like a dope addict. But that's what we began to do. If there was something we could steal, a camera, a ring, a stereo, we'd steal it and then turn around and sell it. And use the money to buy pot.

I had gotten laid off from my job, but the foreman was very kind to me. He called me back when there was work but then there began to be days when I would come in late or not at all. He began to sense that I was having problems, but he didn't know it was because of drugs. I told him that I was having problems with a woman and that was the reason I was always leaving early and coming in late. After a few months, the company laid us off again and I never got called back.

One morning, when my friend and I were getting our money together, we realized that we didn't have enough to fix ourselves through the nose. We had to make a decision. My friend said, "I'm going to skin pop." Which means taking a needle and putting it through the skin, not in a vein. But we didn't do that. I had had a bad night, I'd seen a real junkie, a dope fiend mainline and he looked so cool, enjoying his shot, nodding blissfully all over the place, and I wasn't even half as high from my skin pop. My friend felt the same way. So we went with an older junkie who'd been around for a long time and this was my first experience with mainlining.

I felt the rush come, I felt the warm feeling, the ecstasy trailing off to a calm feeling where you feel and know that the world is arguing and fighting and killing itself but you're at peace. The next day, I did the same thing. Sniffing the stuff meant fifty dollars a day now, and we couldn't afford that. I owed people money, I owed the pot connection money. Suddenly, a few bucks and one injection, that's all it cost. I'd do it just once a day and it felt exceptionally good.

But I was only turning eighteen, I still lived with my family, so I still had to be cool. I didn't want them to find out. About a month after I began shooting up, I was up on the roof. Someone told my brother that I was up there with my friend and this old junkie. My brother came up on the other side of the roof. What happened was that the dope was so good that I started to feel like I'd overdosed. This older junkie was walking me around, pacing me back and forth when all of a sudden my brother showed up. He was furious. "You're trying to kill my brother on me!" he was shouting. The next thing I knew, my father was on the roof and I couldn't keep my senses. I knew I was in trouble. My father was trying to hit me and my brother was trying to hold him off and they were both cursing at my friend. Finally, everybody got me downstairs and there was a family meeting. I just sat there, dazed and sick. Everybody was there, even my brothers who lived a mile away. They were discussing, should I go to a hospital? My brothers knew I was on heroin, but my father thought it was marijuana. And I was just sitting there, and my father would get up and if I said something he would kick me in the shins. Then some of my brothers' friends, some of the older guys from the block, arrived. I was coherent but more than anything else I was still high, very high, and the next thing I knew I saw my mother and sisters crying.

One of my brothers said to my father, "I'll take him. I'll take him to my house and keep him there for a few weeks." The next morning, he explained the rules. What he expected me to do. But that didn't work out well at all. When I went out I said I was just going to go around the block. That was correct. Right around the block to cop. That is when I started hustling in a serious way. That's when I began to understand what a dope fiend has to do to get his fix. He'll do anything he has to do. To begin with, I still had a lot of connections, so the beginning of it was really easy. Suppose someone wanted to cop. I would cop for them. Half a spoon. Half an ounce. An ounce of heroin. I knew the connections. So I would take the person to the connection. I wasn't the type of junkie who beat a guy, who would take the money and bring back nothing but milk sugar. I wasn't at that state yet. For my efforts, I would get my share of dope from the connection.

But I realized that my habit was increasing. Five dollars went up to ten. Ten went twenty. And finally to fifty dollars a day. I couldn't just be a runner anymore. So I began to steal again. I stole anything I could get my hands on. My brothers' things. My sisters'. I stole from people in the neighborhood. I owed everybody in the neighborhood money, but I still had a pretty good reputation from the mairjuana I still occasionally sold, so they knew I was good for the money. I borrowed from bookies I knew but now it was getting to the point where I was stealing hubcaps. The Ford Mustangs, those ones with the wire spokes were good for fifteen dollars apiece, which was good for a spoon. And between Madison and Fifth where I lived, there were two hospitals. It was like my own private turf, where I could do my thing. I used to break into the cars and take cameras. People were always leaving cameras in cars, people who had stopped by to see friends or relatives in the hospitals.

Through all this, I was always trying to get a job, trying to keep jobs, especially ones in a factory. In a factory there was always something to steal. So I finally got a job at a factory that made women's underclothing, which was perfect. You could sell panties, slips, bras and girdles. But one day, I had an argument over how much we were supposed to get paid. The ad said $1.75 an hour, but the boss said $1.25. So this guy and I were so upset that as we left, I picked up a mail sack and took it with us.

Two hours later, I was under arrest. Mail theft. A federal rap. The other guy's mother got him out right away, but my father said, "No, let him learn his lesson." I was in jail forty-one days and then my case came up. I got two years probation since it was my first offense.

Thus, I stayed out of jail until my probation officer couldn't take my line of con anymore, until I couldn't hide the track marks on my arms anymore. When that happened, I was sent to Lexington, a prison that specialized in narcotic cases. When I came out the first time, I went right back to the needle. The second time, the same thing. I was twenty-three and all I'd known for the past five years was heroin.

At this point, it just seemed to me that everything was hopeless. Everything I touched was turning out bad. The dope was getting worse and you didn't know who you could trust. I almost got shot by a cop, and one of my brothers knocked out three of my teeth, roots and all. I had a few close calls. Three times I almost died from overdoses. One of my friends did. He just turned blue and died.

When you're out on the streets, you steal from so many people. You beat so many people. You owe so many people money that you become like a snake. Nobody trusts you. Nobody wants anything to do with you. That's the way it had gotten. And then one of my brothers came to the house. I discovered it was he who had called my probation officer the second time I was shipped off to jail, who told him that I was still shooting dope. It was he who had knocked out my teeth. But when he came to the house, he was starting to get involved in politics up in the Bronx and he said he had found out from one of the Congressmen that there was a program there that worked with addicts and had a religious emphasis. I told him that I really wasn't interested. But he said, "Look, for my sake. For your mother's sake. You're driving your mother crazy."

I decided to go just to see what it was like. It was called Damascus and was one of the first rehab centers. I talked to a lady there and the next thing I knew I was lying on a cot at Damascus and the next day they took me up to a camp near Monticello, N.Y. They had a big home there and the food was dreadful, they didn't have enough finances, but they were really trying. I took Darfines with me, which are pills for withdrawal, and I had enough for ten days. But after the tenth day, forget it. I was too edgy, too uptight, so I left. I just wasn't ready yet.

I had begun selling heroin now and when I came back from Damascus, I got in touch with my connection, who was a very rough customer. I already owed him $200 but I pleaded with him, conned him, and he gave me more heroin to sell. But he said, "Look, we're not going to pipe you, we're not going to send anybody to go after you if you don't bring us the money from this batch. I'm going to shoot you. I'll kill you if I ever see you." He meant it. He was that kind of person. He and his wife were very mean, and this was their income and their life. Both of them used dope and had at least forty or fifty dealers working with them.

In two days, I shot up all the dope instead of selling it. I was terrified. But it was then that I met the guy who told me about Teen Challenge. He was a customer of mine. "I thought you wanted to get away for a cure," he said. But I told him I couldn't go that route. There was no such thing as a cure. I knew that my connection would be looking for me by tomorrow. I couldn't go home. My father had thrown me out of the house, so I was living with another junkie in a furnished room. There were times in that room so depressing that to this day I get sick to my stomach, just thinking about them.

At this time, I was also using another drug along with the heroin. It was called Desoxin. It is used to stimulate pregnant women. On the street we called it "bombitas" and what it actually was was a kind of speed. I had been mixing it with the heroin, which caused me to lose a great deal of weight. I was down to 109 pounds at the time. I was skin and bones. I knew that my connection would be looking for me and I had the telephone number of Teen Challenge. So I made the call.

I made an appointment and went there and saw the place, then I came home. The guy was looking for me all right, so I got my things together and went right back to Teen Challenge. But those first several afternoons I was still conning myself. I kept changing my mind and would run away from the center to cop. One afternoon, as I was leaving again, I ran into Don Wilkerson, who founded Teen

Challenge and seemed to sense where I was going. I waved a casual hello, trying to look cool, and he waved back and said, "See you on the rock." The anger I felt then turned to a terrible loneliness and then a sickening self-pity. As I walked to the train station, it seemed like the waste of my whole life passed in front of me, and as I was going down the steps, I yelled out to God, "Why is this happening to me?"

The night before I left, my friend had given me some dope to shoot up. When I got back to my neighborhood, I went up to the roof and as soon as I stuck the needle in my arm, I heard laughter all around me, like voices saying "Ha, ha, ha, we got you, you're back again. Here's where you're always going to be." I was so sick and depressed that I had no qualms about going back. I came back right away. I came back that night and they gave me another chance. They said, "Go up to your room and stay there and don't come out."

But that next morning I left again. I had packed my bags again and was on my way to the station. But I heard a voice saying, "Go back. Go back." It wasn't a stupendous thing, like Paul on the road to Damascus, but for me it was dramatic because, in all that confusion, God had time for me. Just those simple words. "Go back, go back." So I ran back.

I had no strength. After a few days, in the chapel someone would be preaching, and I would start to cry. I couldn't stop crying, and I would say, God, take away this heroin. I don't want to be addicted. And meanwhile, I just wanted to go back and have a good life. I wanted to smoke grass and go to dances and have a good life. I would tell God, You know, I'm not a bad guy. I used to tell Him that I had a good heart. I never killed anybody and would He just have mercy on me?

Then, in the following days, real tears began to come. I started to go through some difficult emotional changes. I was seeing the guys who were on drugs for just as long as I was, and even longer. I was seeing them change for the better. And I couldn't take the pain anymore. I broke. The flood gates opened and I told God that I didn't want anything if He could just forgive me for what I had done. Have mercy, God, I said, and find something for me to do in this world.

I was almost there now—but not quite. One day, another guy at the center and I snuck out to have a cigarette. At Teen Challenge, we don't allow smoking or drinking or anything of that nature. But that afternoon, we were caught by Cookie Rodriguez, another ex-junkie who worked there and now has his own center, New Life For Girls.

Cookie was very upset with us and said we were running a game on Teen Challenge. He said we should either shape up or take off, split if we wanted to. As I was sitting in chapel that night, I was full of anger. I lost consciousness of the songs and what the preacher was saying because, like a screen lowered in front of my eyes, God started showing me my life before me. As I was as a kid. How I went to Catholic church. How I went to parties. And smoked grass. And dealt grass to children. And stuck needles in my arm. How I lived for those needles. It was a whole disgusting picture that God showed me of my life, of the sorry things I had done. I didn't hear one word of what the guy was preaching.

When he was done, I just went up to the altar and I started weeping before God and that's when it felt like a weight was being lifted off me. And, then and there, God worked a miracle in my life. I had been in a sort of trance at the altar and when I came out of it, a guy named Benny was serving the juice at supper, and I thought, I'm going to tell Benny what happened. But I didn't have to. As soon as he saw me, he looked at my eyes and saw that they were filled with warmth.

"You got saved, didn't you?" he said.

I started to tell him what had happened, but he said, "Oh, praise God!" And that was it. I never had the desire to shoot up again. And I understood how much work I had to do.

LAURA is in her late twenties. She has been an actress, a cab driver and a teacher. Her beautiful, careful eyes reflect the consideration she has given her life.

I was raised a Lutheran, but my parents didn't go to church. Rather, they sent us to church instead. But I could find nothing there from which I could get any kind of spiritual reference or feeling. It was a very dead church, and at the age of thirteen, I simply stopped going. There was no reason to go. It seemed foolish.

My big love was the theater. I won a scholarship to NYU but, instead, decided to go directly into the theater. I had gone to Yonkers High

School, a fine school, and part of my decision was governed by fear. I'd had some emotional problems, based partly on the fact that my mother was an alcoholic, and that as the oldest of seven children, I had retreated into a dream world at an early age. Like many girls, I dreamed of being an actress, of being on Broadway, of being a movie star. As a child, I play-acted in front of a mirror and pretended to be doing commercials and I read plays out loud to myself.

Senior year in high school was when the bug really hit me. I worked at the Yonkers Playhouse. I was property mistress and wardrobe mistress—and it was just theater from then on. It was all I wanted.

I started to study at the famous Herbert Bergoff School and I moved into the city. I lived with my aunt for six months until I moved into an apartment with two other budding actresses. I studied at Bergoff, on and off, for about four years. It was when I was staying at my aunt's, during those first days on my own, that I miscarried on the street. I hadn't even known I was pregnant, and I sat in that apartment, alone and bleeding, for three days. My sister finally came and took me to the hospital. I almost died. I was given three transfusions and God pulled me through.

I didn't do a great deal of theater work. I did do several touring shows and a lot of off-off-Broadway workshops, but I seemed to lack the necessary drive that forces one to press on no matter what. I know now that it was because, all during this time, I felt only empty inside and lost as to who I really was. I had no idea and I was wandering aimlessly in the world of myself.

Then I met a man. He was studying at Bergoff. We fell in love and moved in together and lived together for four years. It was a deadly relationship. A love-hate relationship. I gave up everything. I stopped studying and I stopped acting. I was twenty-one and he had been married and had a little boy and did one show, then got a part in *O, Calcutta!* From then on, his career started taking off.

I was with him through the New York run of *O, Calcutta!* and then we went to California when the show was supposed to open there. That's when I auditioned for the show, to replace one of the girls who quit. But the show never opened in California—the authorities wouldn't let it, because of all the nudity—and we had to come back to New York. Then there was supposed to be a London production, so he went to London and I was supposed to follow him in about six weeks.

When I arrived, I found him in bed with another woman. He had apparently been involved with her ever since he arrived. I went rather crazy after that discovery. I knew no one in London and so what I did was try to kill myself. I attempted suicide. With pills. I didn't want to kill myself. What I wanted was love. Fortunately, I didn't die. But it was only by the mercy of God. I walked into a pub and told some people what I had done. I was barely conscious and these kind people rushed me to a hospital. It was a miracle. God had saved me again, because I should have died, considering the amount of pills I'd taken.

Shortly afterwards, I was on a plane back to New

York and I quickly moved out of our apartment. Just as quickly, though, I was back in the hospital again. I had peritonitis. I was in the hospital for about two weeks and it was then, I believe, that I started my search for an intimate relationship with God.

Because I almost died twice and now I was very ill, I had a lot of time to lie in that bed and think about life, and my life, and God, and my relation to God. There *was* something outside of me, I had begun to understand that. But I wasn't quite sure what it was.

One thing I did was to start to analyze my dreams. I kept a dream diary and then I got very much into para-psychology. After I got out of the hospital, I also discovered psychomotor therapy. It was a type of therapy that employed psychodrama and role-playing and Gestalt. It was a mish-mosh of a lot of things. But then, one morning, I woke up and in my mind I saw an arrow and it was pointing to Boston. I had to leave New York. I think it must have been God's arrow, but at the time I didn't know that.

I knew no one in Boston and the only thing I "had" to do was to continue my therapy, so I packed all my bags, said goodbye to everyone that I cared about, and went to Boston. Through a series of circumstances, I found a communal situation—a big house with ten people—to live in. In those days, Boston was very big on communal living. In our house we had students and some artists and that was fine by me, my morality being what it was then. Then I lived by myself for a year. I embarked on a journey which I thought was a journey towards God, what I thought was God.

I called it mySelf. With a capital "S." Self-awareness, which is all self, but I thought that's what God was. I also did TM and started studying tai-chi. I read a lot of books on Easter thought and was still into psychomotor therapy. I was collecting unemployment from *O, Calcutta!* Because after I came back from London I did a closed circuit taping of the show and was an understudy for awhile. I'd also done the actual show for about two weeks. In the nude, of course, the way everyone did it.

Unemployment was a blessing because, in Boston, I couldn't find work right away and, as a matter of fact, didn't really want to work. I wanted to spend this time in my life exploring the new inner consciousness that I thought I'd found. I became so introverted and involved with myself that I had no friends. I was totally involved in my own world, my own trip. And I realized this wasn't healthy. I decided to go to Goddard College's Adult Degree program, which involved a two-week residence where you worked out a six-month study course, and then you went home. My work would be in the fields I was interested in—the creative unconscious and the way to liberate it.

I now had to get a job; my unemployment had run out. I worked in a French pastry shop for a while, and I drove a cab. And then I discovered an organization called Arica. There were branches all over the country. Someone in Boston had told me about a party in New York which was being given by Arica. And Arica was a school started by a man named Oscar Ichaso, a Chilean master of supposedly everything, from Arica, Chile.

Arica is a philosophy that says that through a variety of exercises—Tibetan yogi, yoga, sensory awareness, etc.—you can reach higher levels of consciousness. It was technological in its approach, rather than spiritual. It assumed that different people vibrate at different levels, and the entire System was based on pride. Spiritual pride. The higher you got, the closer to God you got. Which is the total opposite of what Jesus says. He says, "The least of you shall be the greatest." But what Arica gave me was a tremendous spiritual pride. I thought I was evolving to higher and higher levels. With each level, the bigger the hot-shot I was spiritually.

But none the less, I got sucked into that first party and turned on by a lot of people. I thought they were really spiritually together. I didn't know how I was going to afford the training, which cost six-hundred dollars, but I knew that I had to do it. I went back to Boston and, somehow, I managed to get the money together by borrowing from friends and from my father.

I did the training in Boston. They had a school there and I moved into another houseful of people, all of whom were going through the program. It was an eight-hour day, seven days a week. A variety of exercises, at first just physical ones. Their philosophy was based on body, mind and spirit so, ultimately, each exercise would focus on one of those three. Some would be interpersonal reactions and some would be deep meditations.

We were desperate to have "spiritual" experiences, and I was just as hungry. I started to do drugs at this point in my search for God and I did a lot of acid. I knew there were dimensions beyond the realms I had known, and after I had experienced them I wanted what they gave you without the drugs, without the LSD, the peyote and the grass. I wanted to know God—but to me God was not personal. To me, He was cosmic, was space, the void. He was *satori*. He was Nirvana. He was not a person.

The one thing that I did not have in those days was love. I had a lot of pride, I thought I was very spiritually high, and in some ways, according to their thinking, I was. But I had no love. I was unable to relate to people in a human, loving way. To me, people were just sort of objective numbers, objects to pass by, to leave behind.

I did the training, and then I did the advanced training in New York. It was on this trip that I had my first abortion, which was a desperately lonely and horrifying experience. Today, of course, I would never have one.

I moved back to Boston when the advanced training was done and I began teaching. But shortly afterwards, a group decided to start an Arica school in New Orleans, and I was to be one of the people who was going to be part of that venture. It was December of 1974. I packed up all my things—some people had gone on ahead—and decided to stop off in New York to see my parents before I left. It was the holidays, Christmas time.

Once I was in New York, I remembered that a

friend had sent me a Christmas card saying that if I ever came back to New York to please look him up. He was a man I'd gone out with before I left New York. I called him up and he invited me to a New Year's Eve party, but I told him I couldn't go. I was going to an Arica party instead. I said that perhaps we'd get together another time.

The night of the party I dropped some acid before I went. And at the party I saw the pit of hell. My eyes were opened. I had never had a bad trip before. What I saw was supposed to be what I was after—spiritual enlightenment, a profound awareness. I was aware, all right. All I saw was death and degradation, and nothing that had anything to do with God. The realization came to me in a flash, like a curtain was drawn from my eyes. All of a sudden, the false light was lifted, and the darkness was so dark.

I went home and felt terrible. There was an awful emptiness in my soul. Finally, I called my friend back and he said he'd be right over. After we caught up on our lives, he told me that he'd had a Born Again experience, that he'd given himself to Jesus and he was a totally changed person. It was true. He was so peaceful now and loving and gentle. I knew that he was on to something—the thing that I didn't have, that I had been searching for years to find.

He started showing me different scriptures in the Bible which were in direct contradiction to the things that I believed. "Do not use needless repetition, as the heathen do, for they think they shall be heard for their many sayings." I'd repeated mantras over and over again. That quote seemed to be speaking directly to me. And he read me something from John which said: "I am the door to the sheep." Which meant that there are other shepherds but that He was the good shepherd, meaning, there are other gurus that you can follow, but there's one flock and one shepherd. I am the good shepherd and other shepherds come to steal and kill and rape the flock. And he read me a scripture that said, in effect, everyone who came before me are thieves and robbers. To me, that meant everyone who claimed to be God.

But as he shared all these thoughts with me, I got very confused. I still had all this other information in my head. I didn't know what was happening. But what I did know was that my friend had become very loving. I don't mean in a sexual, male-female way, but in an almost godly, tender way.

I had a plane reservation for New Orleans but I was blown out, exhausted, completely confused. I kept putting off my flight so I could understand what was happening. In the meantime, God did an amazing thing. My father's sister had a stroke, and I had to stay in New York. Thus, I went to my friend's church and again I had the experience of love coming towards me. People were singing hymns and I started to cry. The Holy Spirit came over me and I could not stop crying. I didn't know why and I kept trying to control myself but I couldn't. The tears just kept coming.

But I was also very judgmental of the people there. All I could think of was that they looked so square, so this and that. I knew I could never be a part of a group like this, not if I felt that way. Everybody seemed so different from me, so hopeful and calm.

Every day I went to visit my aunt in the hospital, and I felt very helpless. She was in a coma, and I remembered that people in comas are conscious, that they can hear. So I would talk to her, wanting to do something for her because I knew she was going to die. And on one visit, the only thing I could tell her, I found that I could tell her, the only thing that came out of my mouth was "Jesus loves you." I would sing Christmas carols in her ear which she used to love because she was a pianist. I now believe that God used me to bring the gospel to her on her deathbed, the little bit of gospel that I knew. And one time when I was talking to her, a teardrop came down her cheek and I felt that was her only way of responding.

I went to several more meetings at my friend's group, and I was coming more and more to the conviction that this was the Truth. I started to read the Bible, to look up the things that people were talking about and it started to make sense to me. My aunt died on a Wednesday and Friday was the funeral. That night I went to a Bible study class with my friend. And that night the Lord called me by name. I knew it was Jesus talking. He said I'd come to a crossroads in my life and not to be confused or afraid. That he was my good shepherd, that he was going to save me. And that I had a decision to make.

That was it.

The decision, of course, was, where do I go? Do I

go to New Orleans or stay in New York?

As He spoke to me, I felt a tremendous warmth come through me, the warmth of His love flowing into me, and I knew I had found Jesus. It was an emotional feeling, not an intellectual one. And, suddenly, I was Born Again.

It was an extremely emotional experience. I began to cry again and couldn't stop and it was a feeling of being completely filled up. And I was Born Again that night.

Many times in a believer's new life, Jesus does some miracles to show that it's not all for naught that you've committed yourself to Him. As for me, He immediately got me an apartment. Here I was in New York, a girl with a suitcase and no place to go. But a girl in the fellowship had been looking for a roommate and someone directed me to her. So we hooked up. That's not a miracle, but it was the right time and the right place. Next, I got a job right away working in a day care center as a teacher. With no experience at all. No accreditation and no certification. But they hired me. When I had absolutely no money, suddenly I received anonymously in the mail a hundred dollars. Yet nobody knew I needed the money. I received an anonymous typing course. Apparently, somebody thought I needed to learn to type. And, sure enough, about six months later, I changed jobs and typing was required. And God knew that. He saw that I'd learned.

I think the Lord can work in your life as much as you allow Him to. I wish I could confess a tremendously victorious Christian life since I was Born

Again—but it hasn't always been the case. It's a day by day thing, and surrender. The key is surrendering to Him. And prayer is so much a part of that key. If I don't pray, if I don't read the Word, I can really get bogged down. But when I do pray and the longer I pray, the more uplifted I feel, the closer to the Lord and the more He can work in my life.

FRED is Executive Director of Just One Break (JOB), an organization that helps the handicapped find jobs. He lost his right arm in World War II.

I had an unusual youth. My father did a lot of traveling, and it seemed we lived in almost every state in the Union, except Kansas. During these summers, I learned to ride. I enlisted in the service just before World War II broke out. And though I studied chemical engineering in college, they put me in the cavalry with perfect Army logic.

My basic training was out in Fort Riley, Kansas, and because of my experience with horses, I had the good fortune of being asked to teach a certain colonel's daughter how to ride. Which I did, and sort of became a member of the family. After

I finished my training, I put in for Officer's Candidate School. But I was invited to the colonel's home one night for dinner, and he sat down with me and proceeded to tell me that he was rejecting my application for OCS. That shook me up. I asked him why and, confidentially, he said that everyone who was going to OCS from that post would most likely end up on the Burma Road and they expected at least seventy-five per cent casualties in that operation. He didn't want me to get killed.

Thus, I left there and bounced around to different posts and I ended up with the 2nd Armored Division. This was in the beginning of 1942, and we'd come into the war. We were down in Fort Benning, Georgia, and we spent most of our time practicing amphibious landings. We took "Orchard Beach" so many times that it got to the point where we'd leave half of our equipment on shore, knowing that the next morning we'd be right back on the beach and could pick it up there. Except, one morning, when we woke up and set out to sea we were informed that we weren't taking the beach. We were off to Europe. And three-quarters of our equipment and all our personal belongings just got smaller and smaller as we sailed away from it.

We landed at Fedela, west of Casablanca, in September of 1942. Being in reconnaissance, we were the first to go into Casablanca, and from there we went to French Morocco and Rabat and Fez and stayed outside of Rabat for a couple of weeks. Then we went up the coast to Algeria and, again, we bivouaked for awhile. And then we were called up as support for the 1st Armored Division, which was in Tunisia at the time, and we had a General by the name of Patton. He was a great soldier but a lousy politician and we had great respect for him. Our first major encounter with the enemy, however, was a devastating one. It was at the Casserine Pass and thirty-four of our tanks went in and four of us got out. I was one of the lucky ones.

From there we went to Tunisia and Sicily and then we were shipped to England, and we went in on the invasion of Normandy.

I was heading towards Belgium with reconnaissance when we were cut off. We only had five tanks, and we were cut off from the main body of our forces. They say reconnaissance is supposed to go out and find the enemy. Well, unfortunately, we found it and they found us at the same time. We were stuck on top of a hill for five days, and the entire 5th German Army was around us. They threw everything they had at us.

The day I was hit, all the tanks had been knocked out except the command tank and my tank. My radio was out. Just before dawn, I went over to the command tank to use its radio and I was told to hang tight, they were breaking through in a matter of minutes. Help was on the way. I went back to my tank and just as I reached up to climb back in, there was a tree burst, a shell hit the limb of a tree directly above me, and the force of the explosion crushed my arm from my elbow to my wrist. Since the hatch was open, it killed the rest of my crew inside. The command tank got the next shell and killed all of them, too. I found myself standing around, the only person left.

I took off my belt, put it around my arm as a tourniquet and sat down and lit a cigarette. I figured, well, the war's over for me. My buddies got through in about forty-five minutes and they rushed me to a field hospital where they immediately put me in surgery and tried to patch up my arm as best they could. Surprisingly, my right arm was the only part of me that was hit. The sound, I remember, was tremendous, but I had had a helmet on. They just temporarily patched me up at the field hospital, then flew me to England.

I was hit on July 28, 1944 and by that time I had finished my 362nd day of combat. I got to England on July 29, and they immediately took me to the operating room. I didn't have any definite feelings. I couldn't think that clearly. One of the things I do remember was noticing that they had separated me from the rest of the ward, so evidently they must have considered my case as pretty serious.

The morning of August 1st, the surgeon came to my room. Army doctors were quite different from civilian ones. They didn't mince words. He told me that that morning they were going to operate. They were going to amputate and it was a last resort because they had waited too long. Gangrene had already set in. He didn't think I would survive the operation, especially not the anesthesia.

I was conscious, and I remember thinking that I just wasn't going to die. So I bet the doctor ten dollars.

By a strange coincidence, someone in the administration office of the hospital who saw me had known my father in New York. He decided that he would take a walk up to the ward and say hello. When he came into the ward and saw that the chaplain was giving me my last rites, he immediately turned around and went back to his office and proceeded to write my parents, telling them that he had seen me given last rites and was terribly sorry that I had passed away.

Immediately after amputation, two things happened simultaneously. The first shipment of penicillin arrived at the hospital. It was the kind that came in powder form and you could mix it with alcohol. I got an injection every three hours for the next twenty-two days. At night there were a lot of soldiers in a great deal of pain and the nurses used to come around with trays laden with Seconal, Nembutal and codeine, and they asked you what you wanted. They would give you one of each if you wanted. But I wanted none of it. I had a hunch that if I were sedated, I might die. I simply had never liked pills. And to this day, I think that perhaps that subbornness saved my life.

As everyone does who suffers a loss, be it a part of one's body or a loved one, I went through a period of mourning. I felt sorry for myself. I saw no hope. But it didn't last very long. In fact, within a day or two, I was up and walking around. And in the course of my wanderings, I happened to walk into one of the administration offices during lunchtime when nobody was there. I saw a typewriter with a list of names in it headed "TO BE EVACUATED TO THE U.S." They were at the "B's" so I typed my name in.

By August 20th, I had arrived back home. We landed at LaGuardia Airport and, as we went through customs, I saw a telephone and I called my parents.

My mother answered the phone. I said hello and don't remember if she fainted or not. They had received that letter the day before. I said I didn't know where I was going to be sent, but I did want to prepare them: I had lost my arm. They didn't care, they just wanted to see me. We were temporarily sent to a camp out on Long Island, and their visit was the first time I'd seen them in two and one-half years.

I told them that rehabilitation patients were usually sent to a hospital close to their homes. So, of course, I was sent to Battle Creek, Michigan.

They had amputated just above the elbow and it was still healing. I had some discomfort. Any time you amputate a limb, there are circulation problems, and swelling caused by the blood trying to find new pathways. While I was in Battle Creek, I went into what they call "revision," where the doctors shape the stump and do what they can to put it in condition. And, while I was there, they gave me a three-day pass at Christmas, and I wired back for an extension. And I got it. On the way back from New York, I had an hour stopover in Detroit. While I was at the railroad station, a group of guys announced that the USO was having a dance across the street. They said I should come on over. So I went over to the dance, and that's where I met my wife, who was one of the hostesses at the USO. I always tell everybody I met my wife in a hotel room when I had an hour stopover in a train station, though she doesn't appreciate that. A year later, we were married.

I was discharged in January of 1945 and I decided I would go back to school. At that time, all the universities were on a trimester basis so I was able to start in July. I had several schools in mind but it narrowed down to MIT and Cornell, and I chose Cornell. I had forty-eight months of education due me, and I'd made up my mind to make the most of them. I started studying there and, just before it was time to get a degree, I would drop one credit hour and switch to another major. This way I took everything that interested me—from mechanical to industrial to administrative engineering, industrial relations, psychology and some law. Finally, at the end of forty-eight months, I got a degree. It was an unusual opportunity that most people don't get because I took courses that I truly wanted to take.

I had become accustomed to the loss of my arm. I even found that I could control the reaction of people to me. I could make a person just as comfortable as I felt I wanted them to be. Most people don't know how to react, and the way you react to them gives them a clue. So I found that I could make those people who were antagonistic or for some reason I didn't like as uncomfortable as hell.

Before I was discharged, I had been fitted with a cosmetic arm. But in those days, I still had hope for a mechanical hand. The most difficult thing to learn was to write with my left hand, which took me a good six months. But I began to encounter problems one can't anticipate—and they came in all shapes and sizes. For instance, you are carrying a package in one hand and you come to a door where there's a door handle. What do you do with the package? How do you open the handle? When people shave, they usually use one hand to smear and to steer and the other to shave with. How do you do this with one hand? Or tie your tie? One hand is for holding, the other is for fixing. How do you tie your shoelaces?

All these seemed to me a challenge, and I found that people don't have a hand. They have five fingers. You're not using your hand, you're using your fingers. There's no reason you can't use one or two fingers for holding and the other two for tying. Once you come to this basic concept, you find, as you go along, that things become much simpler. In fact, one of the highest marks ever given, I think, was given to me in pattern-making, which is all mnual woodworking. I wouldn't accept any help from anyone. I loved woodworking and I still do. I have my own shop in the basement and I've paneled several rooms and built a great deal of furniture.

I drive a car. I've driven coast-to-coast. Actually, I had a very funny experience with driving. After I got out of the service, I had to take another driver's test. At that time, I had a 1935 Graham with the old floor shift. I used my artificial limb for shifting. According to law, they noted that I had to wear a prosthesis, as well as corrective lenses. When I got automatic shift in a new car, I wanted this restriction off my license. Any time I got in the car and didn't have my arm on, I didn't want my license saying I was supposed to be wearing it.

I told the Motor Vehicle Bureau that I wanted the stipulation removed. Well, they had every process imaginable to put things *on* your license, but there was no procedure whatsoever to take things *off*. The only thing we can suggest, they said, was to tear up the old license and go out and take a new test. Which is what I had to do.

When I left school in 1949, I met Hank Viscardi, who was just starting Just One Break and asked me if I would like to join him in getting the organization off the ground. I said no, I didn't think so, although I was very interested in rehabilitation. I had studied a great deal of psychology and had been involved in helping with a lot of psychological experiments at Cornell, especially with Phantom Limb. This is a syndrome where the amputee still has feeling in nonexistent "legs" or "arms."

But instead of working with Hank, I decided I would go out and see what I could do on my own. I knew what I was capable of doing and I knew what my educational background was. So I did everything from sales to benchwork to engineering writing. I stayed in touch with Hank on and off, and I was working for Sperry Gyroscope Company, doing engineering writing when I got a call from Hank. He was starting a new company out on Long Island which would employ only disabled people, and he would like me to come to work as his assistant. I told him it was tempting, something I'd really like to do, but I'd have to think about it for awhile.

About a week later, my supervisor said I was wanted in the front office. When I got there, I met the chairman of the board and the president of Sperry-Gyroscope, who said, "Congratulations!"

"For what?" I said.

"We just got the word that you're going to work for Hank Viscardi."

That was the first I'd heard of it. But it must have been a good omen. I went to work for Hank and was his assistant director for both organizations, Just One Break and Abilities. That was in 1954 but by 1956 he was spending most of his time at Abilities out on Long Island, and he resigned as executive director of JOB. I was appointed in his place and have been director ever since.

I think a lot of people become paralyzed by the thought of a difficulty in an opportunity. I like to think of the opportunity in a difficulty. Perhaps this is putting it too succinctly. But I don't believe that disability is a common denominator. I don't believe that just because a person becomes disabled they are any worse or better than they were beforehand. How a person looks at himself is the way other people are going to look at him.

For instance, most individuals have either friends or relatives who suffer some kind of disability. But when they think of that person, they don't think of him in terms of the disability. They think in terms of personality, of the person they know and love. And this is the way I think about disability. You can put so much emphasis on what they *can't* do that there isn't much that they *can* do. And nobody is really interested in what somebody cannot do. In fact, there's nobody who could ever judge what a person can't do. This is something that is immeasurable. It's only what a person *can* do that's important.

When I'm out talking to employers, I try to change their thinking, because most employers, like most people, think in terms of themselves. They think in terms of anticipation: if I had such and such a disability, I couldn't do these things. Therefore, by perfect logic, somebody who has the disability cannot do it. I tell businessmen and the groups I meet with, when you get up in the morning and get dressed, do you tie your tie with one hand or two? Of course, they say two. I say, why? I tie mine with one hand—just as quickly, just as easily as you can with two. It never occurred to you to use one hand because you never had to. Therefore, you can't conceive of the fact that it can be done. How about your shoelaces? Everybody assumes that they need two hands to tie their shoelaces. This is nonsense. I tie them with one. And I also tell them that if you can tie your shoes with one hand, you could tie both shoes at the same time. Look how much time you could save.

This is only to try to change their thinking. And change attitudes. The attitude a person brings to a situation is the way he's going to perceive it. And when you relaize that we're talking about disability, throughout our history, the history of mankind, disability has always been synonymous with evil. The evil one has always been the facially disfigured or the hunchback. Or the man with the limp or the hook. This is how we depict evil and menace. It's the old misconception: black is bad and white is good. The villain wears the black hat. Even today, when there's a mystery on TV, odds are we look for the guy with the limp, the twisted smile. Only recently have we had a hero, like Ironside, in a wheelchair or the blind detective that James Franciscus played.

I make damn sure that, when people come to us, my entire staff receives them as individuals, not cases. Not numbers. Not disabilities. That they take each person as he or she is.

RENEE is in her early twenties. Until recently, she lived in Alabama, which is her home. A skilled pianist, she works for a company in New York which manages concert artists.

I was born and raised in the church, but my first conscious experience of it was when I was five years old. It has stuck with me for almost twenty years now.

It was the First Church of the Nazarene in Jasper, Alabama during a revival service. I don't remember what the preacher was saying, but my mother thought I wanted to go to the bathroom because I kept tugging at her hand. But that wasn't it. "Oh, do you want to go down to the altar?" she said. I wanted to—yes. And I went down to the altar and I said that I know that Jesus loves me.

That's all I remember of that day, but what I said has remained a part of my life ever since. It is my purpose. It's my beginning. And my end. I know that I was conceived of God, I know that I was in His plan from the beginning of time. He put me here for some reason. His will may not be known to me now, or after I die, but I know I'm in His plan.

However, my whole spiritual life has evolved very slowly since I was a young child, so I can't exactly say when I accepted Jesus. But I was fed constantly. My family was a church-going family. Yet after awhile, I began to think that this was all there was to it—going to church and hearing the same thing every Sunday. And it got to be a little boring. Those were my pre-adolescent and adolescent years. But being the "nice" kid that I was, I didn't rebel. I always did what I was told, I never went off the deep end. In a way, I wish I could have experienced something that the preacher was always saying, such as we, as Christians, have been pulled out of the Dark Abyss, the Bad Life. That we should be thankful every day for this. Yet I had never been a bad kid, I told myself. Why am I being told this? I always wanted something to relate that experience to.

I would like to say that I've really been a bad person—before the Lord pulled me out of it. But that had never really happened. Until I went to college. My first year I had a bad time of it because I was away from home and, consequently, got away from the church. It was a time of being alone, of making my own decisions, so I just chose not to be involved with the church at all. And, consequently,

I was not fed anything. I was starved, so to speak. I felt as if I didn't have to account to anybody. But towards the end of that year I realized that that was not what I wanted. I needed the faith that had been constant all through my life. It all came to a head that spring. I realized that I needed God's life. It wasn't just something that was convenient. I really needed it. I was involved with a guy, and I wanted to get out of the relationship and was depending entirely on myself. My own rationalizations, my own assumptions. They were just not enough. He was not religious. He believed in Jesus as the Lord. He believed *about* Him, but he did not believe *in* Him.

Basically, my story is that I thought that I was a rather together person, and I was, as far as the world was concerned. I was knowledgeable about the things that were necessary to get by, to excel. Yet, somebody once said, "There is a God-shaped void in everyone," and I realized this. I realized that I needed it to be filled. It had been filled when I was younger, but I had ignored it. I had starved it of nourishment.

I studied music at Birmingham Southern College. I studied piano and there was another void in me that music filled. It was filled to overflowing but it didn't flow into that particular void. And then I met Richard, the man who was to be my husband. After I met Richard, my whole world changed. I wasn't sure at first where he stood spiritually, but it seemed we knew we were destined. It was one of those immediate chemical things that happen. And we knew that this relationship was going to be very important to our lives. From the beginning, we started out saying that this relationship is going to be in God's hands. So from the first, we handed it over to God. By handing it to God, we avoided trying to run it our own way. It's like taking everything that you are, the two of you, your attitudes, your relationship to each other, your attitude toward the future, whether you get married or not, everything that has to do with you and him, even those things that you don't know about and that might happen in twenty years, you tie it all in a bundle and say, "God, it's Yours. It's Your problem. You take care of it. We'll listen to You and take heed."

One might think that this is shirking responsibility. It isn't. My responsibility is seeking God for the purpose of His will for the relationship. I should add that I try to give everything over to the Lord every day. Sometimes I don't do it, though, because I'm also human and I'm very selfish.

When we met, I was ready to meet a man of the Lord. I had been through the whole bit of being with guys who didn't know the Lord. I knew that a marriage had every potential to be perfect. But I doubted that there was one. But if the man of the house is a man of God, I believed that there was a better chance.

(At this point in Renee's conversation, her husband Richard joined her.)

RICHARD: That summer I meet Renee, I had already received the Lord. And I had made a promise to myself that I wouldn't date anyone seriously unless she was a Christian or became one or knew where I stood. From the very first date I had with Renee, I was determined to see if she knew the Lord. I asked her and could tell by the way she answered, by the tone of her voice, that she was a believer. So that meant things would go a lot smoother, which made me glad. I was falling madly in love with her at the time.

RENEE: Did we lead a contemporary on-campus life? Well, everybody is curious. And curiosity is a good thing. I tried to smoke cigarettes and I was a miserable failure. I'd heard tales that pot was a lot harder to smoke and you really can feel hazy and terrible, too, and I thought, I'm not that curious. At first, I think people smoke pot out of curiosity but then they think they can escape with it. I just did not need that.

RICHARD: In junior high school and in high school, I was unaware of drugs. Most of it was just beer drinking and the only ones that were messing around sexually were the hoods and the motorcycle gangs. So I really wasn't exposed to it. Don't forget, this was the Deep South. And there is still a kind of code of conduct there. In college, I was really not interested in dating a lot. I was more interested in relationships. In college, I started dating a girl who was a very strong Christian girl, much stronger than I, and so as far as sexual temptation and things like that, it never really was a problem.

RENEE: Morals are a very big issue in the South. Oh boy, are they! You just don't mess around. It's not done. You save yourself. I think it's practical. But in my case, it was also a religious and moral thing.

RICHARD: In the South, the church is so tied with the social structure of a town that it's almost the same thing. There's a double standard there. A "good" girl is a virgin when she gets married. A good guy could mess around if he wanted to as long as he didn't get caught. I wanted a good girl to marry, so I didn't want to be a hypocrite. I didn't mess around. For me, it was my mother's influence: some things are right, some things are wrong. As far as religion and what the Bible said, the summer before I met Renee I got to the point where I decided to believe what the Bible said.

RENEE: I came to the city in September of 1976. Richard got here before I did and had met the people of our Church. It is called the New Westside Covenant. Through those people, we got our apartment and met a lot of friends. We started going to this church as soon as we got up here and now we're married. Our religious convictions were re-established more strongly at this church because of the quality of the faith of the people we worshipped with. It was something I hadn't really known before, this deep faith. It has to do with the Holy Spirit. God consists of three personalities, yet He is one. They are God, Jesus, and the Holy Spirit. After Jesus was crucified, buried and was risen again, He said, "Don't be afraid, I'll send you a comforter; I'll send you the person who'll be with you to comfort you, guide you, lead you and direct you. This shall be the Holy Spirit." It's often ignored because just the very words, Holy Spirit, frighten people. They're afraid of it because it is something you can't see. But Jesus said He'd send it and, indeed, a few days later He did. This is the inner strength, this is what I have now that I didn't have before, the comfort of the Holy Spirit, the gift of the Holy Spirit.

The void that I have been talking about has been totally filled with it. It is my source. Or grace, when I'm mad. Or peace, when I'm upset. My source of love when I run out of love for somebody, which happens. My source of everything that I need to smooth the machinery of living and living is not easy without something, and this is the *true* something, the Holy Spirit. There are other things that make life easier, and I'm not a dogmatic person but in this area, the one thing I know and I'll stand on until my dying day: the Holy Spirit is the true reason for living all of life. It is the Truth and that fills the void to overflowing. This is what helps a person maintain his Christianity. This is his direct connection to God.

(Richard, Renee's husband, is also from Alabama. He is currently studying the piano at the Manhattan School of Music.)

Our home was not what you'd call a Christian home in that my father was not a believer. My mother was, but she was not adamant about it. She did want us to go to Sunday School and church if possible. We wound up going to a Presbyterian Sunday School a lot, but we didn't go to church very often.

When I got into the early teens, there was something in Sunday School that kept me there. I benefitted from it, but I didn't know why. I think that God was there and that was what attracted me, but I didn't know it at the time. I just knew it was something, but I got sort of tired of that until I was fifteen and went with some of the kids from the church to a Billy Graham movie. At the end of the film, they had an altar call. That sight shocked me because for the first time in my life I heard in tangible form what the gospel was. I.e., Jesus died for me, a sinner. First, I'm a sinner before God. But that I can have a relationship with God by receiving Jesus into my life just by asking Him.

I had never understood it that way. I had probably been taught it before, but suddenly it was clear as day.

I was terrified, my heart was beating very fast. A girl next to me got up and walked down to the altar. I didn't understand what was going on, yet I knew that's what I wanted. I had been brought up with a concept of God as a personal, intimate being but I didn't know how to effect that. The concept of good and bad had already been brought into me as a child. It made perfect sense. It was simple: some things were good and some were bad. I'd been brought up with absolutes and so, being a sinner, I'd accepted that, too. I was taught that and it made sense. Everything that I'd been taught about the nature of God, as a personality and as a creator with a mind and yet a being infinite, made sense. It still makes sense. I never had any real problem with that.

But at that altar call, I realized that I was separated from this God and there was a way to get with Him. The way was to come forward and confess Jesus as your Lord. I did go down to the altar and Billy Graham's organization had counselors there, and they explained to me in more detail. They quoted the Bible and explained what they said with it. The facts about Jesus. Yet I did not receive Him then.

I was too frightened, too shaken up. It was too emotional an experience, and I couldn't receive Him. But I knew that some day I would.

About half a year later, I was at a concert given by a Christian rock group, and there was the same set-up. This time I knew intellectually what they were talking about and so, finally, I gave in. "Oh, Lord," I said, "I ask you to come into my heart."

At that concert, I had been told that if I asked that in prayer, I would change and there would be some immediate differences and some long-term changes in my life. That I should watch for them.

The first thing that I felt was immediate peace. That shocked me, I wasn't expecting that. And the most immediate result that involved others was that in school I was no longer argumentative. I used to love to argue a point just for the sake of arguing. Suddenly, I had no desire for that. It wasn't fun anymore.

I then learned that the first source of nourishment, especially for a new believer, is the Word, the Bible. But my growth came slowly. I would start to read but a lot of it I couldn't understand, some of it I did. The things I did understand, some of them I didn't like, especially when Paul talked about Christian behavior. It was a bit too much for me. I couldn't conform to it. Not to those standards—such as loving your brethren, turning everything over to Christ. But I came to a point where I started to understand the Bible as truly the Word of God, which was an intellectual decision. I looked for every other way because that was a tough one to swallow. I would see something in my life that was wrong. Gossip, for instance. At one point in college, I was under the influence of someone who was a marvelous gossip, and I loved it. But then I realized this was wrong. It was bad-mouthing people. It was nasty and rotten. So I gave it up to the Lord.

What I said is, "Okay, Lord, I realize this is something that you don't want me to do. Whether it's right or wrong, it's wrong for me. You've shown me that. I like to gossip but as much as I can, I give it up to you. I release my hold of it."

When you do that, something happens inside of you that kills the desire to do it. The same goes for foul language. When I first became a believer, I could cuss a blue streak. But I began to feel bad about it, and I tried to stop doing it on my own. But I realized I couldn't do it. I'd stop for a while, then I'd fall right back into it. Finally, I said, "Lord, will you do it for me? I release it to you. I don't want it." And from then on, I never had the desire to use abusive language again.

It's just like Renee and I giving our relationship up to God. We tied it into a big bundle and released it to Him. And we're free from worry. I release the worry of it to Him. I release my career as a pianist to Him, the direction it will go, the worry. My only responsibility is to listen to Him.

The idea is for the Lord Jesus to be everything, to be my everything, for me to live in Him and grow in Him. But I'm constantly being shown how lacking I am. How short I fall. But it's never "You'll never make it. You're too rotten, look what you've got to live up to." The Lord encourages me. It is a slow process, a slow growth, and it's mainly based on a principle found in Romans, which says, in effect, not to yield my mind and my body to things of sin but to turn them over to Jesus every day. It is a moment by moment thing.

For instance, last spring I found a new insight into the Lord's love for me. At school, I was performing for the first time in front of a jury at a piano concert. I had always been absolutely terrified of playing in front of audiences and, now, especially a jury. But for the first time in my life, I was able to perform three times consistently without any fear at all.

John writes that perfect love casts out fear. I'm starting to realize this and realize that's what it's all about. Renee talks about the God-shaped void and that love is what it is. She's right. That's what it's all about.

*PETE says "I was drunk for thirty-two years."
He is no longer drunk nor has he had a
drink in five years. He is now a successful
writer and photographer.*

I was raised in a Christian home, as a Catholic, and, for a great many years, I drank. I started at fourteen and for all those years I felt the church had closed its doors to me. Like many people who drink, I found myself going less to church and more to the bottle. And if I did go to church for answers, all I would be told was, say this prayer and take this pledge. I would take the pledge and, for a while, not be drunk. But upstairs, in my head, I would be.

I drank for one purpose: to get drunk. Because when I was drunk, words slid off people's noses, homely girls became pretty and I was the life of the party. I felt terrific inside. In my world, things were normal.

I was working as a salesman and I traveled all over the country. I was in ad promotion but what I did for a living is not that important. The fact was that I had a disease and I didn't know it. I was getting sicker and sicker and my life was a kind of nightmare. I was unhappy but I didn't know why I was. And I drank to get rid of the unhappiness which only compounded the unhappiness.

I never really denied God. I know people who drank simply because they had and the guilt was too much for them. Am I a sinner? They drank to make God go away. Or they might say, man created you, not vise-versa. I just sort of ignored Him; we drifted apart. Actually, the more I drank, the more I became God, although I wasn't aware of that. An alcoholic is not always right—but he's never wrong.

You drink, thinking alcohol is some kind of euphoria, but it's not. It's a depressant. The progression of alcohol's effect is cunning, baffling and powerful. It's an insidious disease. It's the only disease that will keep telling you you don't have a disease. My impression of an alcoholic was that of a guy who wore two sneakers, one high, one low, never shaved and drank out of a brown paper bag. And of course, I didn't have any of these characteristics. I was successful in the various endeavors I was in. I didn't see any of this coming. Nor did I see God going. If I got in trouble in any way, He was the first person I'd phone. I'd call God right away and I would bargain. I really didn't know who I was talking to. "I'm in a real bad situation here, God," I'd say. "I need some help." But I would never thank God for getting me out of things.

During this nightmare, a friend of mine was afraid to go to A.A. by herself, and she asked me to go with her. I went and really enjoyed A.A., listening to those funny stories. I thought it was an entertainment. Three acts and a cup of coffee. Cost you two bits. I went for four months. Today I truly believe that that was my Higher Power (in A.A., that is the name that is used to describe one's religious affiliation), letting me know about A.A. Because for me the end was coming. In A.A., I learned about blackouts. Blackouts are a form of amnesia drinking. And I was having them. One night, while trying to find the George Washington Bridge, I ended up in Indiana. It's like sleepwalking, bombed out of your mind. I have no recollection of that night.

I also learned that the end for an alcoholic was one of three things: a cemetery; an asylum; or a jail. Yet it was hard for me to understand that because I was (1) not really listening and (2) I wasn't *that* bad yet. It's only later that you learn to identify.

Yet one day at a meeting, I realized that they were talking about me. I was an alcoholic.

I had become very, very bitter about a number of things, one of which was the fact that the New Jersey courts had said that I was only allowed to see my son fifty-two days a year. Every other weekend. But I couldn't get anyone to listen to me, to understand the love I had for my child. No one understood that fathers can love just as strongly as mothers. I wasn't allowed to see his school records, I couldn't talk to him on the telephone. But I did manage to stay sober on the weekends that I was seeing him. Yet my grief was uncontrollable. The only way to make the grief stop, of course, was to drink more.

Problems were now coming at me from every direction. I was working out of an angry knot, and only drink seemed to make the knot unwind. Finally, the end came. I could no longer stay sober even on the weekends when I had my son. People think that an alcoholic's life can go up and down. Wrong. It goes up very slowly, then comes down like a fist. My blackouts were frequent, hallucinations started. I was up to two quarts of scotch a day and two cases of beer. People know you're not having a party. They know you're alone. You worry about what the garbage man thinks. You don't answer the door. I did eat, and that's probably what saved my life.

I had found a small bar where no one knew me and beer was 15 cents a glass. The day I walked in there, I spent eight dollars and cashed a check for fifty. I felt I had found a home. Shortly after I had discovered it, I wrapped up a motorcycle and I went to the bar, as though it were a hospital. I knew my friends would take care of me. One guy cauterized a knife with gin, and the others lifted me up onto the bar, and he gouged the stones out of my leg. That was the operating table. The next day when I went to the hospital, the leg was infected.

I knew I had to have help at this point. On and off, I would think of A.A. but God knew what He was doing. I think He wanted me to suffer to the point where you grow through pain. You don't grow any other way, and I had suffered enough. I was sick and tired of being sick and tired. I had reached bottom after thirty-two years of alcohol.

I made a call for help. To A.A. I thought I knew all about A.A.; I didn't know anything about A.A. There was a meeting thirty miles away, the woman told me. *Thirty miles!* I won't go thirty miles for *their* love, I told myself. For fellowship and understanding! I want the meeting brought to me! The woman said she'd help me find a meeting that was closer and said, "I'm so glad that you're going." Suddenly, I realized there was someone on the planet who loved me enough to transcend all my audacity, my arrogance. I could tell by her voice that she really cared.

After that first meeting, I found I wanted to go to one the next night. And the night after that. And then I met my sponsor. He seemed to know exactly what was in my head. And through A.A.'s love and patience and understanding, my life started to turn around.

On the sixth day of meetings, I was at home and I hadn't had a drink for six days. I thought, well, I've got this A.A. program down pat. I'm no longer a drunk. But then I began to cry and shake and laugh uncontrollably. It was a nightmare. I couldn't control myself. I didn't know it but I was detoxing, which is like going cold turkey. I had so much **booze** in me that I didn't start to detox for five days. My body was missing something. Why shouldn't it? It was missing thirty-two years of drinking! At the time, I didn't know what was happening to me. Nor did I know all the beauty that was going to open up.

A.A. taught me simple things: *you can't get drunk if you don't pick up the first drink. Keep it simple. Yesterday is a canceled check, tomorrow is a promissory note. But today is hard cash. I can spend today wisely.*

A man once told me if I had a board 365 feet long, he couldn't pick it up, it would probably weigh eight tons. He couldn't even slide it. That's longer than a football field. We couldn't even turn it over. We could do nothing with it. Yet if we cut it up in little one-foot lengths, we can move that 365 feet any place we want. One foot at a time.

For the first time in my life, I started to observe things around me. I'd gone to college and was considered to have more than average intelligence. Yet I had no idea how much brain was there until I started to really use it. And that's not ego. The average alcoholic is clever. He has to be to survive. But now, cleverness was out of the picture. I had to cope. I drank because it made me comfortable. Now I had to replace that comfort with something else. I replaced it with A.A. Their program is physical, mental and spiritual—in that order.

The alcoholic physically must stop drinking to be sober.

Mentally, he's got to straighten out the toy factory, he's got to work on his head.

Spiritually, we come to believe that a power

greater than ourselves can restore us to sanity.

A man I met explained the phrase *come to believe*. First, you come—that's physical. Then you come to—that's mental. And finally, you come to believe—that's spiritual. And everywhere I turned, it seemed someone had an answer that made sense to me.

In A.A., I learned that God was defined as "God as *you understand Him*." It was always in italics. You may believe in a Christian God, you may believe in a Muslim God, or believe in a Baptist God. He is never given limitations. But after about five months in A.A., my sponsor said to me, "Pete, how are you doing with the spiritual end of the program?" And I said, "Well, you've pretty much heard the story. About when I wore a blue suit and a red cape and I ran the universe. Spiritual end? God and I split twenty years ago."

"No shit," he said.

"That's right. Twenty years ago," I said.

"No kidding. Who moved?" he said.

That started me thinking. I began to realize that I had run away from God the same way I had run away from everything else. Had God ever deserted me? Who was it that told me to pick up the phone and call A.A.? Had somebody else gotten Pete drunk? No. Pete had gotten Pete drunk. It was now time for Pete to grow up. I was kidded when I came into the program. They said I was forty-six going on twelve. They were wrong. I was forty-six going on eight. My sponsor patiently told me that it took thirty-two years to forge my character defects. Don't expect to get rid of them in thirty-two minutes or thirty-two days. Besides, he said, you're not going anywhere. Easy does it.

I got my hands on a pamphlet called *Just For Today*. It taught me self-discipline and had some suggestions, one of which was to do two small things *today* that you didn't want to do. I was determined to do anything it suggested. So I washed the sink and I straightened out a drawer full of socks. At the end of thirty days, I had done sixty things that I hadn't wanted to do. I found I could finally organize myself. When I was drinking, any task was so monumental that I would have to sit down and have a drink and think about which thing I should do first.

Physically, I was in good shape; I always had been. Mentally, I was getting better. Spiritually I was going nowhere. I'd try to pray but nothing would happen. But then there came the day when I learned a great deal about God.

A friend of mine held a very responsible job at a big chemical company. He was only thirty-two years old and he'd gone into a hospital for two weeks to detox. When he got out, I took him to a meeting on a Thursday and on Friday he got drunk. Saturday he had a convulsion and on Monday I saw him at a meeting, somewhat bleary-eyed. The following Friday the state police called me. They had found my phone number in my friend's wallet, and they were looking for his wife. He was in a motel in New Jersey and had fallen off the bed. He'd gotten his head jammed between the other bed and couldn't unbend his neck. In a drunken stupor he'd suffocated between those beds.

When the police told me, I was so stunned that I started talking to God. I was very, very angry with God. I said, "You could have given me the right words so Jerry wouldn't be dead." I said it out loud and tears were streaming down my face. I was so hurt that I lost this man who I was trying to help. But Paul, my sponsor, had also heard the news, and he came straight to my house. He walked in, put his arm around my shoulder and said, "Pete, you're not God. This is God's will, not yours." And suddenly, I thought, he's right. If I were God, I could have saved this man. But I'm not. I had to learn what God's will meant.

I had heard a man say, "When you say the Lord's prayer, and you come to the end of it where it says 'Thy will be done,' say silently to yourself, 'not mine.'" I knew what he meant now. It doesn't say Pete's will, does it?

There came a time when I began to trust myself enough in the world to begin to travel. I had gotten several magazine assignments which would take me to different parts of the country, and I was scared stiff. It would be the first time away from home, sober. People at the meetings I went to were also concerned, and I promised everyone that I would take a meeting book with me. There are A.A. meetings in almost every town in America, and the book tells where.

One night in Oklahoma, I encountered a very bad storm. The lightning never stopped. I had never seen anything like it in my life. I turned on the radio and heard that there were seven tornadoes in the vicinity. I didn't know where they were, because local radio stations have the annoying habit of telling you what county they're in instead of telling you what town. I had a road map, not a county map. I saw a state trooper, and he was telling people to go home and get in their shelters, a tornado was coming any minute now. I explained to him that I was from New Jersey and I didn't bring a shelter with me. What did he suggest I do? He gave me a little card that listed six or seven things to do in case of a tornado. Apparently, that was the only advice I was going to get that evening. He meant well, but the little card was the only shelter he had.

It was pitch black now. I couldn't even see the seven tornadoes coming. I got into the car and started driving and I thought, in A.A., when things get too much, they say to turn it over to a Higher Power. They say, let go, let God. I didn't call him God yet. I just referred to Him as Higher Power.

So I said, "Higher Power, I don't know what to do. I can't battle seven tornadoes. Maybe I've battled worse in my life but tonight it's for real. I know you're out there someplace. And I've just started working, I've just gotten sober after all these years. I don't know what to do. I'm turning it over to you. Please tell me what to do." The moment I said, "Please tell me what to do," my headlights hit a sign that said "Rest Area." And I said, "Thanks."

I pulled into the Rest Area and it was the answer. I crawled into the back seat and said, "Higher Power, I'm going to sleep. If you want me, I'll be here." And within two minutes I was sound asleep.

The wind, the roar, nothing bothered me. I knew He was out there watching over me. I knew that now I had two friends. A.A. And God.

That night, for the first time in my life, I felt I had some real support. The next day I started out and headed toward Texas, and there was a terrible accident on the road. Everyone was doing about seventy mph and it was raining gently. The roads were slick. A car lost control, skidded across the median and hit another car—broadside. I was the first one on the scene and parked my car and went over to see if I could help. The person in the front seat of one of the cars looked like he was already dead. It was a very grisly sight. But I heard two young girls, little babies, screaming in the back, so I opened the back door. It looked as though a bomb had gone off in there. The seats were all torn up and these two little girls were on the floor, screaming. It looked as though someone had taken a gallon of red paint and poured it all over them. I picked them up and put them on the grass because I thought that maybe the car was going to go up in flames. Blood was coming out of their eyes, their nostrils, their mouths. I took my trench coat off and put it over them like a little tent to keep the rain off, and I realized how helpless I was and once again called out to my Higher Power.

It was late and the highway was almost empty. Everyone in both cars looked as though they were dead, except these two little girls. I said, "Higher Power, these little girls are going to die. Last week, Jerry died. Then a tornado. Now this. I'm not sober all that long. I don't know if I can take it . . . I need your help because there's nothing I can do for these two little babies. I'm not a doctor. I don't even know where to begin. They're going to die out here unless you help them. Please, help me."

I said "Please, help me" a second time.

Then somebody tapped my shoulder. I didn't hear her come up behind me. But she tapped me on the shoulder and said, "I'm a nurse."

Cynics could say it was a coincidence. But I don't believe in coincidences. Just miracles. A good friend of mine got sober and kept looking for a miracle until one day she realized she found one. She was the miracle.

On the same trip, I came to a city in Louisiana. I had been to this town many times before, but this time I could not, repeat, could not find the place I wanted to go. I've always been able to read maps very well, I've never had any problem. I passed a tourist and visitor's center, figuring only an idiot would go into a place like that to ask somebody how to get somewhere. My ego would never permit something like that. So I drove right on past.

The map I had showed a lake in the town and I used that as my reference point. But I would go down a street, which the map showed as a through street, and it would be a dead end. And I kept being forced out of town. I thought I was going crazy. I kept going around in a big circle, and every time I passed that tourist center again. The third time around, I thought, well, if nobody sees me, I'll go in. I went in and there was an elderly woman at the counter and I said, "Pardon me, I'm looking for this certain street. It seems to be gone." She told me where it was, pointed out my mistake, but I noticed there was something about the woman's voice. She seemed to be trying to hold back tears.

"Are you all right?" I said.

She got all choked up. "I'm awfully sorry. I shouldn't bring my troubles to work."

I spotted a coffee urn and asked her if I could have a cup.

"Certainly," she said.

"Sometimes it's good to talk about your troubles," I said. "I don't mean to be nosy, but maybe I can help."

". . . It's not me," she said. "It's my sister."

"Your sister's in trouble?" I said. "What's wrong? How can I help?"

". . . My husband and I don't even want her to come to visit us anymore," she said.

And then I startled her. "She drinks too much," I said.

She was dumbfounded. "Do you know her?"

"No. I just know the symptoms," I told her.

"She's done everything possible," she sighed.

And I asked her if she'd tried A.A.

"She wanted to, but she doesn't know how to find them," she said.

I went back out to the car and got my A.A. directory and found a phone number she could call. I talked to her about A.A. for almost an hour. The change in that woman's face, the hope that was in her eyes. I explained to her that this was a program for people who want it, not need it. If you want it, you can find it. Finally, I had to go. She embraced me and said, "You've put hope in our lives."

"I hope your sister makes it," I said.

As I left, I turned to say goodbye and she called out to me, "Who sent you?"

"Don't you know?" I said and pointed to the sky.

*KAREN was born in Larchmont, New York
and now lives in New York City.
She is in her mid-twenties.*

I was brought up in the church. My mother came from a Baptist background, my father from a Presbyterian one. I was brought up in a Presbyterian church in Larchmont. We went to India for a year when I was ten and I came back believing in reincarnation, believing that if I swallowed a fly I had probably swallowed someone's mother. I brought back a jumble of Buddhism with me, all unresolved in my mind, not at all clear what it meant or how it related to me. I carried this with me for years.

As an infant, I had never been baptized because, believe it or not, the baptismal robes were in

Holland. They had been sent there for a religious convention. So I was baptized at the age of twelve in the Presbyterian church and confirmed at the same time, but only after I went through a big hassle. The minister would not confirm me because of my beliefs in reincarnation. I would not give them up. He said, all right, then you can't be confirmed in the church. You can't be a Christian and believe in reincarnation. But thanks to my mother, he finally decided that he would confirm me. I wanted to be confirmed. Because all my friends were being confirmed. It was a peer situation. I had very few friends.

I went to church every single day for one month after I was confirmed and, all of a sudden, I thought, well, I don't have to go to church anymore, do I? I'm a Christian now, I've been confirmed. So I stopped.

A lot happened to me between the time I was thirteen and the time I went to college. I met some other people who believed in reincarnation and the occult, and several times I saw their eyes change color, I saw their hair change color when they looked in the mirror. I believed in their power. But people would tell me if I didn't "accept the Lord and repent these sins" I would go to Hell. This bothered me.

Once, walking down the street with a girlfriend of mine, whom I was confirmed with, I was informed that, in a minute or so, she was going to vanish.

"What do you mean?" I said. "Are you nuts?"

"It's written in the Bible," she said. And she told

me about the two women who were walking along and one of them was suddenly taken to Heaven. But I kept thinking, why can't I vanish in mid-air? Why couldn't I go too? These things disturbed me.

When I got to college, my roommate was a Catholic. All my life I had been thinking of converting to the Catholic Church because it always seemed to be the most "religious" of all denominations. So I went to church with her several times. And every single time I went, I cried. No matter what the sermon was about, I cried. I think I cried the hardest when I heard the priest who gave a folk mass at our college. He was a very open, perceptive priest, and he seemed so in touch with the Lord. In his sermon, he said, "Today, in this church, there is someone who is struggling with their life. Today they're going to make a very important decision. They're thinking about it right now and I do hope that they make the wise decision."

I knew the priest was talking about me. I had two decisions I was trying to make, and I think the priest knew that. He seemed to know there was something more that I needed in my life. And that I needed to find it. I knew that if I had a guy in my life, I still wouldn't be satisfied. I needed something that was going to be more lasting, stronger, in my life than just a man.

That day I took communion and, for the first time in my life, it meant something. I felt so full. It filled me up, and I felt I had something I really needed. Though I still didn't understand it.

At the time, I was still very rebellious. I didn't

want my life to change. Yet I wasn't the type of person that would reveal her rebelliousness. I kept it to myself. I lived with it in my mind. Finally, I went to that same priest one night and told him I wanted to join the Catholic Church. He looked at me and said, "No, you don't ... What I want you to do is to go to all the churches in the neighborhood and listen to all the other ministers, the priests, the rabbis ... listen to all of them and then make your decision."

So I did, but wasn't impressed with any of the other preachers. Not the way the priest had reached my heart. So I didn't go to church anymore for the years I was at that junior college. I came back to New York and to the Broadway Presbyterian Church. I felt that I needed a boyfriend and thought, well, I can't just go out on the streets and pick up somebody, so I'll have to join a church. I had been to Europe during the summer and I was upset when a lot of the churches wouldn't let me in because my skirts were too short. They were above my knees, so I wasn't allowed into the Catholic churches in Italy. But that trip to Europe provided me with what I consider a minor miracle.

One day, while the girl I was traveling with and I were wandering around Florence, I saw the most beautiful cross I had ever seen in a shop window. It was very simple, and very elegant in its simplicity. I knew I had to have it, but I had left my money back at the hotel.

The next day I went back to the store, but the store was gone. And I was on the wrong street. But I didn't know the name of the street I should be on. I knew that by the time I could find the shop the little gold cross would be gone. I walked all over Florence that day, completely lost, and finally I said to myself, well, I'm just not meant to have that cross. I went into one last store, almost as a reflex action, and there it was.

It's the cross I wear today.

At the Broadway Presbyterian Church, I did meet a young man who became my boyfriend. We went together for a year and a half. I enjoyed being with him. He was satisfying that side of me, yet in my heart I knew that he wasn't the right man to live with or marry. I was going to the New School for Social Research and teaching kindergarten to support myself. I was very active in church activities, yet I still felt a real emptiness inside of me. It was a spiritual emptiness. I seemed to need an assurance that no human being, no amount of social contact, could give me. What I was searching for was a strength that couldn't come from man. It had to come from someone more powerful.

In 1972, I attended Castleton State College in Vermont for my B.S. degree. There, I learned about a Christian youth group. I remembered seeing a sign that said "Christian Fellowship," and I thought I'd look into it, though I couldn't remember where it was held. I knew it was in my dorm but I just didn't know where. I walked into the first floor rec room and there was a whole group of girls sitting on the floor, playing cards and drinking beer. I cleared my voice and said, "Can you tell me where the Christian girls are?" They looked at me and broke out laughing. They thought I was crazy. They said, "Oh, you must mean Marilyn. In 119."

I thanked htem and knocked on 119. The girl called Marilyn invited me in. I said, "Are you the Christian girl?" She looked like she didn't know what to say. But, finally, she said, "Yes, I am. I am a Christian." It was almost as though she was afraid to admit it. As though both of us were guilty of something. As though this was a war and we were the underground.

Soon after, during dinner, another girl asked if anybody wanted to go to hear a Christian rock group called the Keystones. I said, sure, I'll go. We went and the group reached me like no other group ever had. There was something about the way they were singing. A spark seemed to begin to grow in my life. I had a car at this time and on a Friday night—I remember the date, Oct. 19th—the Castleton Christian Fellowship was showing a film. I watched it and tears flowed out of my eyes. It was about a yearly Christian conference at Urbana, Illinois. That film really hooked me. As I watched it, I said, "Okay, Lord, I know you're up there. And I know what I'm searching for. What I'm searching for is you. I want to go to Urbana next year, but I know I can't go."

Then somebody asked me, "Why can't you?" And the answer that I gave her was "Because I'm not a Christian."

In actual fact, you didn't have to be a Christian to go to Urbana, though at the time I didn't know that. What I really meant, I think, was that I didn't want my life to change. I was still afraid. I didn't want to be born again yet—but I did. My soul cried for it. But I knew a drastic, traumatic commitment was needed. And I knew I had to accept the Lord. But I thought, I can't! I can't accept him! I can't become a Christian! Why? Because it would mean giving up myself! If I was going to walk with the Lord as He would have me, I'd have to totally give myself to Him. In the future, if the Lord showed me something that I was doing that was wrong, a sin I was committing over and over again, I would have to stop for the Lord! I had to be willing to give it up for the Lord! This would be impossible. I could never do it. I believed in reincarnation. No, I didn't. I didn't know what I believed!

"Oh, Lord," I said, "I want to become a Christian tonight. I'll do whatever you want me to do!"

Tears were in my eyes. And as I drove home that night, I said "You know what's in my heart more than I do, Lord. I ask you, is there anything I have to give up before I ask you to come into my heart? Will you tell me what they are?" I waited several minutes and then I said, "All right, Lord, I think the time is now. I give you my life."

I took my hands off the steering wheel a moment—I'm not sure why—and then I put them back on and kept driving.

I had been on the way to my parents' summer house in Benson and when I walked in I said, "Mom, Dad, I want you to sit down. I have something very important to tell you . . . You know how all these years I've said I was a Christian? Well, I was lying. I don't know what I've been."

"Are you now, dear?" my mother said.

"Yes."

"Well, what happened that's changed you?"

I looked right at her. "I accepted Jesus into my life."

My parents were stunned. They started to leave the room.

"There's something else," I said. "I'm not going to be here over Christmas. I'm going to a Christian conference in Urbana, Illinois."

"How much is this going to cost?" my father asked.

"One hundred and twenty dollars," I said. "And if I can't pay for it myself, I'm not going."

My father looked at me. He knew by the tone of my voice that I meant it. And that I was going. In fact, I even paid for another girl to go. I saved up. I knew the Lord wanted me to go. My parents had no real objections, but I'd been through a lot of phases and I think they thought this was just another one of them.

Urbana '73 was terrific. It was a missionary conference for people ready to go out in the field. Some of them had been Christians for years while others weren't Christians in the Born Again sense but had accepted the Lord through years of devotion.

A lot of it was over my head. I spent most of my time reading the Bible from cover to cover because I had never done that. In many ways, going to Urbana taught me the discipline that was needed to turn one's life over to the Lord. So much study was needed, so much reflection, yet all for the purpose of action, for the purpose of serving the Lord.

I stayed at Castleton for two more years, from 1973 to 1975. I was very active in the Christian Fellowship, yet even though I had the Lord, there was still something that was missing, and I didn't know what it was. Then one day in December of 1974 a Christian brother who was active in the fellowship came to me and said, "I've been praying about this for a long time and I really think this is the Lord's time for you."

"Time for what?" I asked.

He was insistent that I be baptized in the Holy Spirit. He was a Pentecostal Christian and that sect believes that if you're not baptized in the Holy Spirit, you're not fully a Christian. This disturbed me because I knew I had accepted the Lord.

"If I accept the Lord, then I'm a Christian. That's what I've always believed," I told him.

"I'm going to baptize you in the Holy Spirit. Right now," he said.

"You do that," I said.

He put his hand on my head and started praying in a weird kind of language that frightened me.

"Go on. Talk," he said. "Just relax and talk. At first it will sound like baby talk."

"I don't want to. I can't," I said.

"That's the Devil talking. Relax and you shall speak."

I was terrified. I started making up some nonsense sounds just to chase him away. But I was shaking when I left my room and went down to supper. My friends could see that something had happened but they didn't pressure me to find out what it was. They knew that when I was ready to talk about it,

I would tell them.

I struggled with what this guy had told me and read the scriptures to find out what the Lord had to say about it. Soon the Lord told me to talk to someone about what had happened. I had become depressed. Nothing seemed to cure my depression. So I went to one of the girls in our fellowship and told her what had happened. She couldn't help me, she said. So I went to another girl. What I really wanted to do was to rebel and go to a party that night but I felt the Lord did not want me to go. He wanted me to have answers. So I went to see Marilyn in 119, who had become a good friend of mine.

I told her what had happened, then found out something I hadn't known before. She was also baptized in the Holy Spirit, she spoke in tongues. But she wasn't a pushy Christian, she wasn't the type to chastise me. All she did was quietly explain what talking in tongues was, that it was written in the Bible, and there was nothing to be afraid of. All you have to do, she said, is to ask and wait.

That night I went to my room and asked the Lord, "If there are any reasons why I shouldn't be baptized in the Holy Spirit, Lord, would you show them to me?" And, gradually, I began to relax and felt like I was floating on a cloud, and I began uttering a language that I had never heard before. I seemed to be making sense, although it didn't make sense. But I knew that I was worshipping the Lord and that was something that meant a great deal to me. I understood that you didn't necessarily have to pray in tongues. It was simply another road to the Lord. Some Pentecostal Christians believed you did. But I learned that the Lord doesn't always want the same thing for everybody.

After college, I got a job as a housekeeper in an old people's home. My mind had again become quite confused and distorted, this time due to a girl I went there with. We were both dissatisfied with the churches in the neighborhood because it seemed to us they weren't preaching the gospel according to the Bible. So we weren't going to church very often. And I felt this was wrong.

There was one church that was fairly good and I went there from time to time. There was also a service on Wednesday night and, one night, I didn't particularly want to go—but something said I should. At the service, the elder said, "For some reason or other, I feel the Holy Spirit is asking me to say this... When I was searching for the baptism of the Holy Spirit and trying to understand what it really meant, I talked to a great many people in the neighborhood. Well, they've all moved out." And he sat down.

I thought, what on earth is that supposed to mean? I sat through the whole service, which was maddeningly dull, then went up to him and said, "Excuse me, but where did all those people go?"

"Some went to Maine. Some went to Northern Vermont," he said.

"How long does it take to get there?" I asked him.

"Four or five hours."

"Aren't there any closer?" I asked him.

"There's some in Massachusetts."

"How far is that from here?" I said.

"About an hour or two," he said. "It's called the Living Gate Christian Center."

If the Lord wants me to go, I thought, I'll be there.

That Sunday I piled into my car and drove there and went through a series of intense talks with the minister. He told me to leave my job immediately and go back home for a while. He helped me to understand my fears, to have faith in my belief in the Lord. He said that sometimes a frantic search for a stronger faith is actually an evasion of the faith one has. He said I had a gift. I was either of the Lord or I wasn't. And I was.

I went back to New York and began attending fellowship with a group called One Flock. Some of us spoke in tongues, some didn't. I met my boyfriend there and it's been a full, joyful relationship. We praise the Lord together.

I know that since I have accepted the Lord, it's really meant my life. My life has been better. I've had struggles and there have been times when I've been battling things that I should not have had to fight. Sometimes the spiritual battles are twice as difficult once you've accepted the Lord, which can be hard to understand for those who have not experienced the struggle of His glory. I also have an assurance now that even if I don't make "it" in life, it's not going to be the end of the world. I'm not going to die. My life will still be alive because I have the Lord. I know that I've done a lot of things that are wrong, that are sinful. But I know that, even if I do them again, if I ask the Lord for forgiveness, He's going to give it.

CHARLIE is sixty-three. He was Born Again in 1934. He is his own one-man religious crusade, distributing tracts and preaching The Word at his own Brooklyn church.

I was married at nineteen and it was rough because it was the Depression and we had no money. I've been married to the same woman now for forty-four years. I've got two lovely children, two lovely in-laws and four beautiful grandchildren. I couldn't ask for anything better. But shortly after my marriage, I was so depressed I wanted to commit suicide.

I depended on my father's farm to make a living, but when I went to my father and mother's house they didn't treat me well at all. Therefore, my wife got piqued. She would say something nasty about my mother, and I would hit the roof. And then a fight would begin.

I suppose I had gotten married to get away from my parents. But when you are nineteen, you don't know the consequences, you don't know what a marriage is. You start with a dream but the dream is too fresh, too young, and fighting comes into the picture. It began to get like a nightmare. And I wanted to kill myself.

I was so desperate that I stole my brother-in-law's revolver. He was a cop. I went to his home on his day off, climbed through the window and stole it from him. I was going to shoot myself through the head.

But I wanted to think about it for a while. A few drinks would loosen me up. Then I'd do it. I went to a bar to do my thinking. I had never been drunk before this but that day I had twenty glasses of beer. Naturally, I was feeling no pain. I was very happy, in fact. I said to myself, suicide? Shoot myself? Who wants to kill himself? I never felt better in my life.

Until about after my eighteenth beer. Then I felt awful. And out of nowhere someone came along and started talking to me about Christ, our Lord. I said, Boy, if anyone needs Jesus now, it's me. So he sat down and talked to me about Jesus, and I listened.

I was fortunate because my wife had an aunt who knew all about the experience of being Born Again. I went to her house and saw the contrast. The whole family was Born Again, and they were all singing hymns and seemed so happy and they were enjoying life. They weren't fighting and yelling. Then I went to another aunt on my wife's side, who also had religion. Plenty of it. But they were all cursing and swearing, and they were angry, mean people. What a contrast. And I said, I want what the other family has. So I went back to her house. It was September 16, 1934. I went back to her house and I began to cry. I said, "Lord, take the Devil out of my life. Save me, Lord. Come into my house."

Within half an hour, the spirit of Christ, the Holy Spirit came into me. I knew it because there were about fifteen people in that house and I kissed and hugged everyone, and never in my life had I been so happy. I had been happy when I married my wife, but on our wedding night, the first thing she had done was open up her Bible. My wedding night. And she started reading psalms to me. I never knew what a Bible looked like. I never read a Bible. But I was a very faithful Catholic. I went to church faithfully. I loved the Catholic mass—but I felt nothing. I had no joy. There was no peace. There was nothing. And that night of our wedding, my wife started reading me the 23rd Psalm. Who wanted to hear poetry? Who wanted to hear it? I wanted to get to bed!

After that day at her aunt's house, I began to feel something I had never felt before. Love came into my heart, and it was a kind of love I had never experienced. Friends would say, "Hey, Charlie, what happened to you?" Because I used to curse and swear and cheat and lie. I used to beat up a Jew every day because he was a Jew. I was a guinea bastard, he was a shinney bastard. I hated niggers, I hated Jews. I hated the gypsies, I hated the chinks. I hated. I hated. Yet I was known as "a real nice guy." But the more I read the gospel, I began to understand that it was only Jesus Christ and the Word of God and the Holy spirit which could bring peace to a troubled heart, that it was Jesus Christ who brings the only true good news. I learned that he died for me and rose again, that he ascended to Heaven and that he'll be back.

He's going to make this world a beautiful Kingdom. If you're a Protestant or a Catholic or an Episcopalian, you say, "Our Father, who art in Heaven, hallowed be Thy name, Thy Kingdom come . . ." People are dying to have a kingdom. All over the world, the educated and the uneducated, they are dying to see peace and humility and love. They want to see righteousness on earth. But there isn't any of this at all. There never will be through the efforts of man. Only through the Prince of Peace, the Lion of Judeah, through our Lord, Jesus Christ.

When Jesus was at the Garden of Gethsemane and the soldiers came, they took a sword and chopped off the ear of one of the servants. And Peter drew his sword. "Peter, put back your sword," Jesus said. "He who lives by the sword shall perish by the sword." And when he was on the Cross, he said, "I could call a legion of angels." But He came to die, in order to give us redemption.

We know the Bible says "God so loved the world that He gave his only begotten son that whosoever shall believe in him, shall not perish."

How old is God? What's His age? He's from eternity to eternity. But it's not enough that we know that. It's not enough to know God in your mind. You can *know* all about him but if you don't receive Him in your *heart,* you're nowhere.

Being Born Again was what I needed. Every human being has a nature that is no good. People say that through the prophets of science and education we will have a better world. It isn't true. Human nature is wicked and cunning and very foxy. Even people who think they are "good" people, who donate to charities and sponsor Little League teams, these are the ones who will stab you in the back if it benefits them. You can't depend on human nature, but you can trust in God. God tells us that our natures are no good. And you'd better believe Him. The world has gotten no better and it will not get better until Christ reigns on this earth.

I am two people now. I have been since September 16, 1934. I am the old man, and I am the new man. The new man wants to see the world have peace and tranquility, he wants to see happiness in all lands. He has grandchildren and he loves them and wants a good world for them to go forth into. He knows what God can give. God loves to shower us with blessings but we don't let him.

There was the time my father said, "Charlie, he's an imbecile. He says he's found religion but what was he doing last Saturday night? He was playing cards." At that time, some people considered it a sin to play cards. Or to go dancing. Or go to the movies. But my philosophy is this: if I can play cards with you and talk to you about the gospel,

I've got something wonderful going.

I have a brother-in-law who doesn't go to church with me anymore. His sister once said to him at a party, "You know what? It's a sin to drink wine." He looked at her, had about four more glasses and hasn't been to church since. And he is still unsaved. All because his sister didn't know what she was talking about. It happens when you don't understand what God is trying to teach us. A glass of wine now and then or with meals is healthy as long as you don't overdo it. How can someone go around telling people a glass of wine is a sin? And this was my sister, who was Born Again several weeks after I accepted the Lord. If we are taught properly in the Lord, we can grow and mature in love and understanding. Not only can we help ourselves, but we can help others.

When the Lord says, come to me, He means it. When you come, you don't have to be religious. He's saying, you've tried everything else, well, try Christ. Some say He's a blasphemer, an impostor. But I'd rather believe that He's telling the truth. Because you have the greatest joy on earth if you accept His Word. His Word gives us victory in this world. We don't have to die to go to Heaven. We have it right here. We feel it in our minds, we feel it in our hearts. What has God prepared for us? In my Father's house, there are many mansions. I shall prepare a place for you, that where I am, you shall also be.

When he came to New York City, I gave a Bible to Fidel Castro. I gave a tract to Kruschev at the Hotel Biltmore. I sat with Billy Graham at Yankee

Stadium. I gave my tract to Vice President Nixon—yet all I ever graduated was elementary school. But for seven years I went to Bible school and because of Bible school, I learned the Word of God. I also learned the isms, the cults, all the doctrines, but what I really learned was the Word. And the Word is God. And God is Jesus Christ and the Holy Spirit. Separate them, try to divide them and you've got nothing. Just like our government— three branches. The legislature makes the laws. The executive sees they are carried out, and the judicial punishes. God, the father, He made the decree. God the Son paid the price, and the Holy Spirit punishes. In the Bible it says, there is only one place where you will never be forgiven, in this world or the world to come. You can be a murderer or an adulterer. David was an adulterer and a murderer, yet he was forgiven. He wrote the beautiful Psalms. But God says, all manner of sins shall be forgiven except the blasphemy against the Holy Spirit, which shall not be forgiven in this world or the world to come.

I was in Kansas City once at a religious convention, seventy-thousand people, all denominations, raising their hands, praising the Lord, singing Hallelujah, and I am sure that He smiled when He heard that sound.

GEORGE is in his late twenties. He is a shy, delightful man who has dedicated his life not only to God but to nursing.

I'm originally from Teaneck, New Jersey and grew up in a traditional Protestant family. We went to church on Sunday, and I went to Sunday School. The church was definitely a part of my life. At times, I remember it as a very meaningful part of my life. But at other times, I remember being struck by things that were said in church which seemed foolish, odd. Sometimes I wished I could go someplace else on Sunday.

If "religious" means church-going, then my parents were "religious." As far as actual experiences of knowing the Lord and living with Him day-by-day, I think my mother comes closest to that. I know she reads devotional books and prays, and I think she has real contact with the Lord. To this day, I'm not sure about my father. I know he goes to church, that he has served as an elder and does certain things with the church. But I have never really been able to talk to him about his religious experience.

I'm twenty-seven now, but five years ago I had the experience that began to change my life. And it came about through a great deal of despair. I was going to college at Drew University. I would go to church because I liked the college chapel which was very different from a traditional church. Drew was a Methodist school but it was not a particularly Methodist service. So I was dabbling in its energy and fellowship. I was also majoring in philosophy and taking a new interest in psychology, and I had the feeling that perhaps I was sort of outgrowing religion. I would pray, God was still part of my life but it was an on-and-off thing.

I felt that I had reached a crossroads. I was either going to go one way or another. The "other" would have been to do what ninety-nine percent of the people do, spend their lives doing their own thing and trying to build a life that's easy and comfortable. And that's all there is to it. Some of them go to church and some of them don't. But I was at the point where I wanted to seek the Lord, I had a real need, because I had been incredibly depressed for months. I had a complete paralysis of the will. I would say, gee whiz, I *should* get going, *get* ahead, *get* through college, but I just didn't want to do any of it. Nothing seemed worthwhile. Every thing seemed pointless. And I felt terribly anxious all the time. I kept thinking, I can't get myself moving. What's going to happen to me if I can't get myself moving? Everything's falling by the wayside.

I had spent the summer working in a mental hospital, which was incredibly rewarding, and now that I was back on campus I would figure out all the world's problems and solve them all. But I came back and, suddenly, nothing made sense. School work didn't make sense; I could do nothing useful. Friendships fell by the wayside. I did have a few friends who were religious "freaks" and one good friend who was in theological school. He was an interesting guy, and we had terrific theological discussions. He had caught fire with the Lord and had started a prayer group. I'd drop by his room occasionally and he would tell me about how he was saved.

Saved? I thought. He must be some kind of wierdo. Yet I liked him. He was my friend. He talked about things that weren't cool to talk about. I could relate to what he was saying. I was in awe of his intensity, the intensity of his entire life.

It was a Friday night and he and some other guys invited me to a house fellowship. I didn't particularly feel like going, but I had nothing else to do but stare at my walls. We got in a car and drove for awhile and then we came to a house, an ordinary house. I walked inside and there must have been forty people there, the house was jammed. The analogy would be that it was like a wild party, everybody turned on, smoking dope, but it wasn't dope. It was the Lord. Everybody seemed to love one another, and there was such an air of peace in that room. When someone spoke about sharing the Lord, I felt so at home. I remember thinking, you think you're a Christian. You're not sure but, obviously, what these people have and what you have right now are two very different things. I felt a conflict building up during the course of the evening. I began to want to say to myself, either go with this or stop teasing yourself with the Lord. And I didn't want to stick with what I had. You've got to go after what they've got, I told myself. It was a completely selfish kind of thing. It wasn't an altruistic love of God. It was: I want their trip, not the one I'm on.

It's not that I was a tremendous sinner. I wasn't robbing or stealing. I didn't feel hypocritical either, because I didn't know anything different. I simply didn't think of my life as something that I had turned over to the Lord.

That's what we talk about when we talk about the Born Again experience. It's one thing to go to church once in a while, to live a good life, but to actually talk about dying in your self, the self you were born with, the self that wants to look good and be cool and do normal things, to actually start asking the Lord to open up and give you a second birth, it's not a casual thing. It's terrifying at first; it's saying to the Lord, okay, you take over my life. I surrender.

At that party, I asked people to pray for me. And then they spoke to me about what it meant to be Born Again. So I said, okay, I'll turn my life over to the Lord. They prayed for me to receive the Holy

Spirit and, as I was thanking the Lord, strange sounds came out of my mouth. I found out I was talking in tongues.

At that same meeting, I watched my emotions, waiting for something magical to happen to them. But nothing did. I still felt depressed. I said to the Lord, Lord, you've done something in my life anyway. I'll just kind of lay back and wait. And hope.

I talked to Dave, my theological student friend, and asked if I had received the Lord correctly. I wondered if I was doing something wrong because I hadn't really had an emotional experience yet.

Several months later, I was working in the mental hospital again because I was a conscientious objector to the Vietnam War. I had a dinky little room and felt pretty miserable, but I was still searching for the Lord. I was reading a lot of C.S. Lewis. I went down to the laundromat one day and was reading Lewis' *Mere Christianity*. I was sitting there, waiting for my clothes to be done, and I looked out at the sky and, all of a sudden, the phrase "you are accepted" just came to me. I suddenly realized—in this depression I think I'd seen myself as the Lord saw me—that all the good things I'd done, tried to do, were really just my own ego trip. I was trying to look good to get myself to feel good. But I saw that God, seeing me and knowing exactly where I was at, saw right through me. Saw me the way I was and, no matter, accepted me, and loved me. It was the most incredible, fantastic experience I can imagine. A great warmth spread through me. Through my arms, my legs, and into my heart. It was unbelievable; it was a revelation.

The first thing I did, I went back to my room and in a corner was a pile of books that I'd borrowed from the library. They had been overdue for months. I simply hadn't been able to return them. It had become a thorn in my side. I just hadn't been able to return them. There they were, just sitting there. And the longer I hadn't been able to, the more guilty I felt. It had gotten so bad that every time I walked into my room, I couldn't look in that corner. Now, the first thing I did, I looked in that corner and it was so easy. I called up one of my friends and said I want to return those books. Tonight. He came over in his car, drove me to the library, and there was no problem at all.

After that, I went through a definite swing as far as my emotions were concerned. It wasn't altogether healthy. Whereas before I had been depressed and you could barely budge me, now I was nothing but energy. I only needed a few hours of sleep and work was a sheer joy. During this manic time, someone suggested that I should see a doctor or get into some kind of therapy. So I joined a group therapy session. But I made a bad mistake. I kept telling the group that everybody needs something outside yourself. You can sit there and rap about the problems you have, what made you that way, et cetera, et cetera, but that you are still stuck with the same self, the same problems, and you have no power to change them. It's only through the Lord and His power that you can change.

I wanted to share my rebirth with them. But I got

blasted. And I don't blame them. I was too gung-ho. I was completely insensitive. I didn't have the patience to understand their point of view. I was trying to convert not only the group but the doctor.

It was ironic. Here I was, just beginning to be Born Again and healthy and whole, or so I thought, when actually I was disturbingly manic and very freaked out. After trying to convert the doctor for several weeks, I decided the best approach would be to talk with him alone. Of course it was of no use, but I was undaunted. I thought, wow! this is what I'll do. I'll go down to the psychiatric hospital where he works. I'll sign myself in, if necessary, and corner him there. And that's what I did. I went down there and waited for him and spent some time playing my guitar, singing songs and entertaining some children who were in the waiting area. And I prayed for awhile. But when the doctor came down, he wouldn't talk about Freud versus the Lord. He said he'd called my parents and they were coming to get me. They were going to put me in a mental hospital for awhile, not this one but another one. He said he had diagnosed me as being manic.

Although, at the time, I didn't want to go, my three months in the hospital were a good experience. I think it was probably the Lord's way of slowing me down a bit. But it's hard to know if you're crazy or not. I suppose it depends on what your goal is. If you're looking to change the views of a psychiatrist, yes, you're crazy. But if you're looking to follow the road the Lord has chosen for you, you're not crazy. My experience has been that the Lord shows you one step at a time. And you follow that. As you see one thing, you'll see other things starting to unfold. Soemtimes you have an experience and say, how come, Lord? Why did this work out this way? And you never find the answer. Maybe we never do until we get to meet the Lord.

My stay in the hospital was absolutely involuntary. I was very angry when I got there. This is not fair at all, I thought. But I decided I had to train myself to put it to good use. Even with the thorazine they gave me, I still needed very little sleep. I'd go to bed at ten o'clock because those were the rules, but I'd be up by four in the morning, which was beautiful because of the time I had to spend with the Lord. And gradually, he began to show me how manic I had been. The feverish energy. The mile-a-minute speaking. The frantic single-mindedness. And when I would pray, He would tell me to relax, to try to relax and cool it. "This is where you are right now," He told me, "so why not obey the rules?" And after that, I started becoming a good patient. Then one day, I received a shock. "George," they said, "we're going to discharge you." Discharge me? What had I done? I thought. It didn't make sense. I was the same man. Or had the Lord gone out of my eyes?

After I got out, it was hard to find a fellowship that I could feel comfortable with. I was out of college now and I felt lonely, but I spent time alone with the Lord, read the Bible and sought the Lord in day-to-day life. I was working in nursing homes as an orderly and went to nursing school part time. This was in 1974 and once again I felt as though I had come to a crossroads. I needed to find a body of Christians, a new fellowship, but I didn't know where, so I started looking. I read something about a University Christian Fellowship on a bulletin board at the Presbyterian Church on 114th and Broadway. I was living in the city now. I took the subway but it was the wrong one and I ended up walking across Harlem to get there so I arrived late. It turned out to be a kind of discussion group—people rapping about what "a college education is supposed to mean." So I said, "Well, Lord, let's try somewhere else."

I went back to the dorm and mentioned that I was looking for some Christian fellowship and a friend said, "Hey, George, there's a guy down the hall who's into that." I went down the hall and knocked on the door and who should it be but Dave, my old Born Again buddy!

He told me about the group he was going to, and the next week he took me with him. Again, I felt that these people were really onto something. This was a different set of feelings. I had been alone so much. It had just been me and the Lord. But now I felt as though He was beginning a new experience with me. I would be part of a body, a Christian body, which we started to become. Not just a group of people who met from time to time, but a group of people who wanted to become a church. I knew this was the way I wanted to go. It was the highest form of dedication.

My life began to change. I had a friend now. Dave was right down the hall from me and was one year ahead of me in nursing school. Any time we'd have a problem, we'd go into each other's rooms and be able to talk about it, pray about it. He was kind of like a brother in a way. He got married a year before I did, and he was best man at my wedding.

I finished nursing school and now I am accredited. I love the work though I wish I wasn't so clumsy—I'm still not a man who's very good with his hands. I love my patients and I try to take care of them and make sure they feel comfortable and that, while they're ill, they are at peace. The good thing is that I know I have a calling for the work.

I have a wife now, Louise, and I never thought that I'd be so blessed. God is so alive in both our lives.

When I wake up, I wash my face and shave and before I get dressed, I come out into the living room and spend some time with the Lord. The first thing I do is give the entire day over to Him. If something particular is on my mind, I mention it. Recently, I mentioned a job interview. Would He help me to be straight-forward? Would He help me tell them of my weaknesses and my strengths?

LOUISE is in her mid-thirties. Her association with the Lord has taken her to the deepest interior of Brazil. Currently, she works as a secretary in New York City. She is married to GEORGE, whose story has preceded hers.

I was taught to say grace at the table. I was taught to say the Lord's Prayer at night. I went to Sunday School, and it was a waste of time. I wanted to understand, but I was only six. But when I began to get older, I started to understand and, after awhile, I knew more than the teacher. This was in the Episcopalian church. And then I was confirmed, which meant you were supposed to receive the gift of the Holy Spirit. But nothing happened. Nothing happened. I wanted the experience of God that I expected to get. But I didn't.

In that church, at my age, which was twelve then, if one quit Sunday School, there was no youth program to enter instead. By that time, one was supposed to know all one needed. I didn't think I did. So I started going to Sunday School with my Presbyterian friends. I enjoyed that. At least I respected my teacher, and I became active in their youth program, too. By the time I was a senior in high school, I was the president.

I still hadn't experienced the Lord then, and I wanted to. I was very lonely. Church was the only place where I had friends. Some of my friends had had a real experience with the Lord, and the fact that they had gave me hope that I would, too. After awhile, in that small upstate New York town, I forgot about it.

But not for very long. I went to a district youth rally, and a man spoke about his experience of being Born Again. I was impressed with him and went home and did what he suggested in regard to receiving the Lord. My loneliness seemed to go away, and I believe I was Born Again then. It wasn't very traumatic or very emotional, but I felt a lot more settled and satisfied. I was seventeen.

I talked to my youth leader and my minister about what had happened, and my minister asked me to talk about my experience to the congregation. Episcopalians usually don't talk about being Born Again, and I thought my parents would be upset, since I hadn't told them what had happened. After I agreed to talk to the congregation, I had to tell them. They weren't happy about it. They let me finish out the school year but after that, they said, they didn't want me going to the Presbyterian church anymore. They thought the Born Again experience was something I should get over as quickly as possible.

I went off to college and didn't kick up a fuss about my parents telling me where to go church. I wasn't going to be around that much and as soon as I left, I would worship where I wanted. Through college, I continued to pray and feel closer to the Lord. I visited quite a few churches but didn't settle into any particular one. For awhile, in my senior year, I dropped the whole thing. I wasn't sure I believed in God. And that feeling was to have a body but no heart. That year, I also got very depressed. I could barely make it to classes. I wasn't talking to my friends. And I almost couldn't graduate because I couldn't finish my thesis. Finally, a different friend each night would pray with me, and I began to gradually come out of it. This wasn't the first time that had happened, but it was the worst.

During the summers of my junior and senior years, I had worked as a counselor at a Christian camp. That first summer, I had also gotten depressed and was going to leave. The camp director told me that I could go, but she wished I would see a friend of hers first. Her friend came by and told me that the depression was caused by demons. She took authority over the demons, she said, and told them they had no longer had power over me. I believed her. I suddenly felt fantastic. I stayed that way for three months and managed to stay free and at peace as long as I believed that she had gotten rid of them. But after I got back to college, after some people cast doubt on what she said she'd done, I lost faith again, and my depression came back.

Toward the end of my senior year, a friend who had been Born Again the summer before insisted I go to a meeting with her. I didn't really want to go but she practically dragged me, and after the meeting I went right home. She realized I was gone and came back to my house. I didn't want to see anybody and I wasn't going to let her in, but she insisted. She stayed outside the house, calling to me. Finally, I opened the door. Her words broke the cycle of depression.

Not long after, I was playing the piano in one of the dorms, waiting for a ride home because I lived off-campus. There was no music there except a hymnal, so I started playing "Just As I Am." It became real to me. After a while, I stopped playing it and I prayed it instead. I didn't cry, though I felt like it. The hymn says "Just as I am, I come to you." And I did. And I knew He was here with me and that He had accepted me, in spite of everything I'd been through.

Part of my confusion had been: what am I going to do now? I was a liberal arts major but what could I do with that? I still felt too shaky to think about graduate school, so I took a six-week course in teacher education. I had no previous experience but at the time you could take a cram course and then receive a provisional state license. I got a job teaching second grade in Glens Falls, New York, and went to school in the summer to finish up my degree.

Meanwhile, I came in contact with some Pentecostals. My friend who had prayed with me when I was so depressed was a Pentecostal, and she suggested that I accompany her to a two-week camp seminar. I wasn't sure. It would either be terrific or it would be awful. I decided to give it a try anyway; I felt the Lord wanted me to go.

The strangest thing to me, which I'd never seen before, was that the Pentecostals all worshipped the Lord in their own ways, out loud, at the same time. They spoke in tongues; some of them praised the Lord in English, some in German. I thought it was weird and said to myself, no thank you. God's not the author of this confusion. What did I get into here? I wasn't sure I wanted anything to do with it. And I was upset for three days because I had been so sure the Lord wanted me to go. But after two or three days, I decided that if I'd been right in the first place the Lord did want me to attend. I had better settle down and find out why.

Esther, my friend, had told me that the director's wife was a good person to talk to about the Pentecostals. I decided that was a good idea and all one day I tried to get up enough nerve to go see her. Which was a very mature thing for a young woman to do, wasn't it? I just couldn't bring myself to go see her. Finally, that same day, at dinner, I decided I had to grow up and stop all the procrastinating. But the director's wife solved the problem for me. She saw me and called me over on a pretext, and then explained to me the reason people speak in tongues: to praise the Lord in a language you didn't learn, one you don't really understand, either. You don't pray. Your spirit does. In Acts II, it says that at Pentecost the disciples had been gathered in fear, behind closed doors, and they were filled with the Spirit and there was the sound of rushing wind and appearances, tongues of flame, and they spoke in tongues, they spoke in other tongues and people from all over were gathered in Jerusalem for a festival. They heard them praising the Lord in their own languages and then Peter preached.

After she explained this, I told her that I wanted to be filled with the Holy Spirit, and she and her husband prayed with me to that end. Again, this was not a particularly emotional experience but I did feel the Holy Spirit. I didn't speak in tongues but that didn't seem to matter much, they weren't the kind of Pentecostals that push it hard. All I did was relax and enjoy praising the Lord.

For several months, I went through a lot of frustration because all of my friends were speaking in tongues—so why wasn't I? Then I decided to forget it. I didn't want it. I didn't need it. One night when I was at home, praying for a friend, saying, "Lord, I don't know her needs . . ." all of a sudden, the Lord said to me, "Well, if you don't know her needs, I do. Let me pray through you." And I began to pray in tongues for my friend.

I taught children for three years and after that I went to Bible School at the Bethany Fellowship in Minneapolis. Bethany is a missionary school, and I believed that the Lord wanted me to be a missionary. It is a unique organization, a communal fellowship that has been in existence longer than most. There are about one hundred and fifty adult members and one hundred students. They support themselves by making camping trailers, electric drills, and publishing books. The students pay $150 when they prove they are serious about being there. Then they work and don't pay any room or board or tuition for the four-year program.

I really enjoyed my year at Bethany. I intended to be there for four years, but at the end of my first year I saw a note on the bulletin board: Would anyone like to go to Brazil to supervise kids in a correspondence course? Location? The interior. Missionaries, after the four years, usually go through six months of orientation, plus a year of language school. I kept being attracted to the notice, but I said, that's ridiculous. I'm supposed to be here for four years. I made a joke of it at the breakfast table, and one of the students said, "I think you should pray about it. I don't think it's a joke." So I prayed about it and asked for what I thought was an impossible sign.

Bethany's policy is that their missionary candidates approach them; they don't recruit. They wouldn't approach anybody and say, "We think you should be sent to Brazil." I prayed and said, "Lord, if you want me to, please have a staff member approach me." Which I knew was contrary to policy. That same day, I went to work and a staff member I knew said, "Louise, can I see you a minute?" They weren't suppose to call us out of work either.

"Are you thinking about going to Brazil?" he said.

"Why?" I asked.

"Because I heard what you said to Jean at breakfast." He told me that ever since they'd gotten the notice he had thought that I was the one who should go, though he hadn't felt free to tell me until he'd overheard what I'd said that morning.

I went through the application process and ended up going to Brazil. It was almost on the border of Paraguay, in the state of Parana, a very, very remote place. I flew down alone and I landed in a strange country. They were supposed to come out from the interior to meet me, but they didn't. They had an American from San Paulo meet me and put me on the right plane to the interior. I was quite lonely for a while as I was the only singel girl at the mission station. There was a Bible school program so there were single Brazilian men at the station but at first I didn't speak Portuguese.

Teaching was a satisfying experience. There were very few kids so it was an individualized teaching situation, and I really liked the language study. I was tutored in Portuguese and the language fascinated me.

I got to know people who knew the Lord much more emotionally than I did, and I was impressed with the spiritual depth of some of the completely uneducated Brazilian people. Here, I suppose, we would call them "natives." There was a delightful Bible student whom I loved to go calling with. She couldn't write her own name, but she taught me a lot about being able to pray with faith.

In Brazil, evangelism was an accepted thing. When we went calling and knocked on doors, we would always be asked in and offered a cup of coffee. They wouldn't necessarily agree with us but they would take the time to listen.

I stayed in Brazil for three years. There was a hitch to that as my contract called for two years. At the end of that time, we'd discuss whether I was to go back to Minneapolis and Bible school. At the end of two years, I prayed about it and I believed that the Lord wanted me to go back and finish school. I told the fellowship that, but the international director misinterpreted my letter and wrote back saying how glad he was that I wanted to stay on until they could find a replacement. And the Brazilians said that they really needed me, they didn't think I should go. I felt trapped. And I also said to myself, where did I miss the Lord's guidance?

A few months later, the international director came by on his annual visit, and I talked to him. He said he was terribly sorry for the mistake, that I didn't have to stay if I didn't want to, I could leave on the next plane if I wanted. He and his wife took me on a vacation so I could at least get out of the interior, and I prayed a lot about what I should do. It ended up that I filled out an application to stay, to be a permanent member of the mission, but then the director said, "No, I think you should finish Bible school." And I said, "Enough is enough. I don't know who's hearing the voice of the Lord, if you are or I am, but one of us isn't." So I came back to New York City instead of Minneapolis and Bible school.

An uncle in New York offered me a place to stay until I could find a job as I didn't want to go home.

I found one in an employment agency and my own place to live, also. Then I answered an ad for a job teaching in a Lutheran parochial school. I was still very lonely; I had never had a man. It seemed I was always without a man.

Teaching had begun to get to me. I had been doing it this time for two and one half years. And I had gotten depressed again to the extent that my teaching was affected. So I quit. I got a job as a mother's helper with a family in Connecticut and they gave me a sense of place and, being a Christian family, a place to go to.

And then I met George. I met him at the fellowship I had started attending. Shortly afterwards, I moved back to New York and got a job as a secretary and gal Friday. And George and I got married.

When I get home from work, George is often there because he works different hours, and I feel really grateful to the Lord for having sent him to me. It's a real wonder because I had given up the idea of getting married, of ever having a man. I'm glad I waited for the right one.

When I wake up in the morning now, I'm not always aware of the Lord but by the time I'm fully awake I'm ready to meet with Him. Usually, I read the Bible. Recently, I've been looking for the character of God and for ways to praise him. I underline passages and then read them back, such as, "Lord, you are my shield and my rock and my salvation."

HOWARD is a psychologist with his own private practice. Previously, he was one of the first directors of Phoenix House. A vibrant, athletic man, he speaks passionately and with insight about his six years as a junkie.

I don't think my childhood was unique. On the surface, there did not seem to be many hardships. My father had a business and there was always enough money to buy us things. I have an older brother and a younger brother, so the family stayed together and was a family. If there was a lot of dissension, it remained among us.

My role in my family was that of the middle child, which, I think, had a great deal to do with my getting into drugs. I was the peacemaker; I would take care of the different members of my family.

That way, I got some recognition and love. I was supposed to be the glue because, in so far as emotional health, my family was not together at all. One might say it was falling apart . . . and I was the glue.

One example of this was that I had a brother seven years younger than me, and I had discovered that my father and mother had not been happy about having another child so late in life. Thus, I got a lot of points, a lot of credit for taking care of him, for being "good" to him.

Also, as long as I remember, my mother had been a highly strung, desperate woman, constantly despairing about what was going to happen to her, what was going to happen to her if my father left her. And I was her confidant. My role when I was with her was to appease her, to calm her down. I was given a sense of importance by this role and it also put me in a focal or central point. I got a lot of attention. However, in order to play this role, I had to be in control of my emotions. I wasn't allowed myself. In the midst of all this trauma, this upheaval and need, there wasn't much time for *me* to need. I could need but the way I would *get* would be through my ability to care for people. To be pleasant. To be nice. And, therefore, as a young person, aspects of my personality were never really developed.

I grew up in the East Bronx in the 'fifties, which had gotten to be a very tough place with a lot of gang wars. A lot of families were concerned with their image. They were mainly immigrants and to be immigrants could be terrifying. They came here, imagining a kind of Nirvana, but it wasn't. My parents were immigrants, and they, too, were concerned about being accepted, which filled me with a feeling of wanting to be accepted, along with the feeling that I would never really belong. That I didn't belong. Only recently have I come to accept the truth that I don't belong, and I do. But that's my sensibility. I've always felt that I was an outsider. Yet, if there was a group of people I admired, I wanted to be part of that group. I would do what I could to become part of it. A good example would be the first drug program I entered. There I was, a junkie for almost seven years, getting off six, seven, eight, nine times a day, but when I heard of a *group* of people who did this and were trying to stop doing it, that was the attraction. A group existed, and I wanted to be a part of it.

One never knows what all that family stress can do to you. It gets to the point where one thinks, has it happened to me, am I its victim? Or did I create it?

I was an athlete, and in high school, I was a three-letter man. I didn't know anything about drugs, I didn't see drugs and wasn't even aware of them. My biggest activities were playing ball and occasionally going out drinking with the guys. I went right from high school into college because it was the thing to do. It was what my family wanted and what all my friends were doing. But I didn't do very well in college. I couldn't maintain a C average, and they tossed me out after a year and a half. I went to work as an office boy for CBS, and to City College at night, and I did phenomenally well. I had better than a B average.

I went into the Army in 1959 for six months, came out of the Army and went back to college. I graduated two and one half years later. I went back to college because, while I was in the Army, I had started to read. And it opened me up. I had never seen anyone in my family read a book until I came home with an early Harold Robbins novel, and my mother started reading it. I had never seen my brothers or my father read. The books that deeply affected me in those days, that I feel ultimately pushed me out into the world, were Kerouac's *On the Road,* Hesse's *Sidhartha,* and Fitzgerald's *The Great Gatsby*. *Sidhartha* suggested that there was an ultimate goal in experiencing life; Kerouac was out there, seeing life, and the symbolism of *The Great Gatsby* showed me that here was a guy, with anything anyone could ever want, looking out across the bay, at this imagined, romantic love of his. It showed me that The Quest is pointless, yet every man must follow one.

I had been going with one girl for four and a half years. When she broke up with me, I was crestfallen. Perhaps the relationship wasn't going anywhere. Perhaps I pushed her away from me. But the interesting thing is that the week she decided to end it, I smoked pot for the first time. I remember going to see her that last time. I had six joints with me. "You don't want that," she said. "What are you doing with drugs?" She took them from me and threw them away. This was my last year in college. And at my final exams, I took a bennie. Drugs were all very new to me. And I was starting to hear a lot about mescaline and then LSD. Leary was up at Harvard with his International Fraternity for Eternal Freedom.

After I graduated, I came into the city and started to hang around with a Broadway crowd—the old mambo scene and Birdland. I was smoking a lot of reefers and taking a lot of mescaline trips, perhaps two or three times a week, and I had started taking a lot of pills. Uppers. Downers. That fall, 1961, I played my last football game.

I had moved to West 57th Street into a three-room apartment that was a sort of clubroom for between fifty and sixty people. I thought they were the swingingest, happiest, partyingest bunch of people I'd ever met, and I wanted to be part of this crowd. I was having a ball. There were junkies coming in and out, but I didn't give it any thought. Yet, at some point, I started to see through the crowd. It became transparent that these people were extremely unhappy. They were musicians, salesmen, social workers, heiresses, playboys, hustlers, pimps—a total Manhattan spectrum. But I understood why I wanted to be part of that. Because they *laughed*. They were "with it." We were dropping pills, taking a popper there and there, and it was all very clique-y, all very chic to be getting high in New York at that time.

I was into hard drugs within six months of graduation and I had a needle in my arm. It was a very swift transition, this passage from being a comparatively straight guy to a young man of twenty-three who craved heroin. But, as I've said, I wanted to be part of the group, because they were such happy, fun-loving people.

I was living in this apartment and one night I had a date with a beautiful little Jamaican girl. She was stunning, and we were talking in my room. A friend of mine was also there. We went out to the living room and there was another girl there who was snorting some heroin. Louie and I had never tried heroin, but he said, "One time. That's it." "Solid, Louie. Me, too," I said and we both took a one-and-one and I went back into the living room to this beautiful girl. I was in heaven. I loved the feeling. I felt it underneath my fingernails, in my toes, behind my eyes. And it felt fantastic! But there I was in bed with a beautiful girl, and I wanted to make love to her—only suddenly I didn't have any drive. I didn't have any need. A couple of hours later, I left the bedroom, went back out into the living room and got some more. It as almost as if I was hooked from the first moment.

In those early days, several friends and I would split a three dollar bag and get very high, by snorting it. Then, after a while, we couldn't do that. It didn't get us high enough, so we would each buy our own bag and, in no time, we were all shooting it. Friends of mine on 33rd Street had a set of works, and I shot it with them. It didn't seem very traumatic. The first time I had ever shot anything was cocaine, and it didn't do a thing for me. To stick a needle in my arm again, I just didn't ever give it any thought. I thought beyond that—what I was going to get out of it. Thus, it really didn't seem like a big thing to move from snorting heroin to shooting it.

There was one moment, I think, where I made the choice to become a junkie. I was in therapy at the time, seeing a shrink three times a week, not knowing what I was seeing him about, knowing that my parents were paying for it. I'd tell him about what I was using, what I was doing, and he'd keep telling me, "You're a junkie. You're addicted." At that point, I would get high, then not get high for four or five days, then get high again. About a year after I graduated from college, I had started driving a cab. I decided I wanted to tell the shrink that he was right, I am a junkie! And I almost did. By now, I had a steady cab driving job, and I had a steady income. I wanted to go ahead, I wanted to become a junkie! I *wanted* to have junk every day. So I did and I stopped seeing the shrink. I made the conscious choice to do it. I stopped battling myself because I really wanted it, I liked the feeling.

It is interesting what they say about heroin. It didn't affect my mind at all. It was my stomach I had to calm down. That's what it did, it calmed my stomach down. I learned that my stomach is where my emotions come from. It's the gearbox. So I was taking care of my emotions that way. Which was to numb them out, to bury them.

In the daytime, the life of a junkie is an incredibly emotional one. You're constantly on the fringe. Whether you've got all the dope you need or not. If you do, you're walking around with a certain paranoia because you're illicit, illegal, you're doing something wrong, so there's still a churning going on no matter how much junk you've taken. If you haven't any junk, you need some, and that anxiety, that desperation will cause you more stomach trouble.

I drove a cab for three years, plus I hustled, plus I would sell pot, plus I would scheme and I would burglarize. Or I would forge things. The heroin affected me physically—but never in terms of my looks. I weighed perhaps twenty-five pounds less than I do now. I didn't look too bad because I am a big guy. The only real loss was a lot of my teeth, out of neglect, and I think because of the milk sugar which is used as a cut.

As my life as a junkie continued, I began to get busted. The first time was in 1967, for possession of drugs. I had been stopped in the street, and they found drugs. It was obvious because I was a white guy in a black and Puerto Rican neighborhood. You didn't see a white man there unless he had "business" in the neighborhood.

Other times, I got busted for stolen credit cards, grand larceny, and passing checks. The interesting thing was that I always got myself busted. One time I broke into an apartment with a guy and we couldn't find anything to steal. On the way out, we saw the super and he said, "What are you guys doing here?" And we said, "We're going to visit the Smiths but his door is broken. It's wide open." My partner left in a hurry. But the super said, "What do you mean? Show me the door . . . We've got to call the police." And I said, "Oh, I'll call the police." Before you knew it, I was arrested.

Another time, I was in a department store, using a stolen credit card that belonged to a priest. I didn't steal it, I obtained it. Working this department store was a fulltime job. I would go in, buying things on order for people. I was there at least five hours a day, taking the stuff out, putting it in a locker downstairs and going back. But after about a week, I got to be noticed. Finally, they arrested me—but I made a big escape. I was in the security office, and I saw all these exits, so I knocked several people down and ran to an exit door, which had a big bar across it. I got about three or four blocks and then they got me.

I was constantly getting parole and probation. I never seemed to spend much time in jail. A month. Two months. So when I got arrested this time, they got me for violating probation and this time the probation officer had had it with me. He told me either to get into a drug program or I was going to another kind of program for one to three. I tried to get into Daytop Village and went to their induction center for about two months. But they told me I was incorrigible, that I would never be rehabilitated. I was working the East Side bars at that time, and I was a hustler: how could I stop using drugs and still live out on the street? I would make the meetings. I would go to the groups. I would do what I was supposed to do there, but that was only four hours a day. There are twenty other hours. And I was not able to keep it together. I knew I was going to jail, I was due in court for sentencing, so I left the country and went to London.

In London, I found a doctor who would prescribe whatever I needed. He said, "What do you use? Heroin? Cocaine?" I said yes. I had never used much cocaine, but he began to give me seven grains of heroin a day and six grains of cocaine. All pure stuff. And I wouldn't use the cocaine the first day, so it was just piling up, but now that I had all the drugs I wanted and I had them all the time, I was bored. So I started to mix the heroin and the cocaine and, within a month, I was down to 135 pounds.

I could not feel the heroin anymore; I was using so much that I would use a week's supply in a day and a half. I'd just sit at a table, pumping it in, pumping it in. And, in between, nod out or be exhilarated or go to Picadilly Circus and sit under the statue there, feeling my heart pound away. I OD-ed a few times but people pulled me out of it. What happened next was that I'd switched doctors, but the new one wouldn't prescribe cocaine. So I forged it. One time I did such a bad job that I even used colored ink. I brought it to the pharmacist, and I saw him going to a different place than the one he usually went to to fill the prescription. Instead of leaving, I went into the bathroom, took a monster fix, came out and just stood there. Even there, I supervised my own arrest.

I did a month in prison and then they deported me. I told myself that if I got through Customs and they didn't lock me up, I'd turn myself in. I knew there had to be warrant out for me. And that is what I did. I turned myself in. The probation officer thought that was significant and gave me another opportunity to get into a program. I went to Daytop Village again, went to their meetings for two months, and again they threw me out and told me I would never make it. I hadn't gotten heavily strung out again, because I'd had it. In London, I'd had the junkie's dream. All the dope I needed. And I knew it wasn't the answer. But I had started up again while I waited to get off the street. But in the back of my mind I was going to kick if only to get the probation rap off my back. Ultimately, after Daytop turned me down, probation told me I had ten days to get into another program of some kind or it was the slammer for me.

There was a new program just getting started called Odyssey House. Eventually, they took me in. Somehow. Because I didn't even maintain all of my appointments. In the back of my mind, I was only going to go there for a couple of months just to get the pressure off. And then I'd come out.

A junkie's ego isn't much of an ego. He lives like a pariah, an outcast. On a lovely, spring day, he walks down the street and looks at all the people and says to himself, look at them, they're feeling good, they feel nice about themselves, and look at me. He feels he doesn't belong. I felt that emptiness, too. Something was missing in me. It wasn't an overwhelming feeling, but it was there. I used to let it be known that I was junkie. I played off it. I hustled from my misery. I would go into some of the East Side bars, let's say at noon or one o'clock. People knew me, and they'd see me, sweaty and clammy, and they'd say, "Already?" And I'd borrow twenty dollars which may or may not get paid back. Or in one place I was the day bartender, so I would steal the bank in the morning, go out and get my fix and make it back during the day. Of course, I got fired. Being a junkie, it's graphic, you're demonstrating your pain. You are saying, *I'm miserable, I am unhappy, I want to kill myself.* But you don't. You're doing yourself in, but you don't. It's a power: a victim is a very powerful person. He sucks everything in. That is also why it is a difficult role to let go of. How many times did I say to myself, I want to stop using?

When you really want to, you do.

I was totally disgusted with myself. Also, what happened in the last few years of my life as a junkie was that my image of myself as a hurt soul began to change, both in the straight world and in the world of drugs. If I would go and buy junk and somebody would beat me, either in regard to the junk or physically beat me—I would get somebody else to feel sorry for me and help me out. Or I would go back to the East Side and moan and groan and hustle more money to buy more drugs. I would even hustle my parents. They knew I was junkie, and I even manipulated them through their terror of my getting hurt or locked up. I would mention that I had stolen from stores and, because my father was afraid I might get shot, he would give me money.

But the last few years, I found it more difficult to get the money. And if someone took advantage of me or beat me up, I could just not allow that kind of reputation to exist on the street. I fought back. It was really my first assertiveness training. I had played a lot of football, so there was always the capability for violence in me. But there was also this "Mr. Nice Guy" image that I had superimposed, that came, I suppose, from learning how to survive with my family, from being that considerate, take-care guy, which I had to lose to some degree in order to survive in the world that I had made for myself.

I was desperate now. It was getting more and more difficult to obtain quality drugs. The police were getting wise to drugs; undercover informers were everywhere. It was harder and harder for me to get the money for drugs. I had burned out a lot of my sources. And the trip to England had spoiled me; I hadn't had to get out on the streets. For awhile, I hadn't had to be a criminal.

Finally, I went to the FBI with my father and said, "Look, I'm a junkie. Can't you fix me up with a doctor so I can get it legally?" They said no. Then I went to one of the original methadone programs but they turned me down because I'd only been a junkie for five years, and I'd only been arrested four times. They wanted junkies who had been shooting it for ten years and had a long record of arrests. I kept searching for some way out, some authority to give me shelter, yet not totally believing that I was ready to stop.

But there was no shelter, no relief where I could have it both ways. I went into Odyssey House completely strung out. I had to kick my habit cold, which was something I had done every time I was arrested. There was no medication, nothing. What they did do was to keep me very busy, working all the time. Odyssey House was just being formed at the time. And something happened there. I had just turned twenty-nine, and I had made a vow that I would kill myself if I was a junkie at thirty. What happened there was that I began to see a first ray of hope.

In those days, all the program had was one-family house on East 109th Street. and we were in the process of building what is now the Odyssey House headquarters on East Sixth Street. So we would commute every day for almost two months. There were eighteen of us, living in this little one-family house, on triple tier beds, and they allowed me to sleep in the middle bunk because I was kicking then, and they didn't want me rolling out of the top bunk.

What was so good about the program for me was that there was a structure within the work, a chain of command. The newest people always started on the bottom. And they made sure I got no preferential treatment in any way whatsoever, that I was treated just like anybody else, which was good for me. I could not manipulate, I could not con, I could not scheme. It was difficult for me and, at the same time, because it was hard, it had value. If it had been easy, I don't think it would have had much importance. The court system, the probation department, were easy. I could manipulate them. So I never really had any faith in them.

In the program were people who had lived through the same experience as I had, and I couldn't bullshit anybody. Being a bullshit artist of the first rank, they were extra aware of me. The idea of being ordered to mop the floor and clean the toilets was incredible, yet the next day there was the guy who had told me to do it expressing the same feelings I had had in group therapy. That was truly amazing to me. The idea of getting together and being honest with one another, no holds barred, with the opportunity to release what was happening, to discuss it in openness, made me think that not only was that good for me, but that, through this program, we could change the world. And it was then that I began to see a future for myself.

After I was there for forty days, I had my first probe, where the senior members probed you with a lot of questions in order to decide whether they were going to keep you or not. I was so scared because I wanted to be kept. It was a surprising emotion because forty days earlier I was thinking, I'll get there, then I'll leave. I wanted to stay and during that probe I told them that if they threw me out, I'd sit on their stoop. Somehow, I wasn't thrown out. They let me stay. And we grew together, and I saw myself part of something that was dynamic and growing. We would talk about getting bigger and handling more people and getting better facilities. I felt that the information that was being run on me and the other guys had a certain truth ot it. A simplicity. Helpful sayings like, what goes around, comes around. What you put out, you get back. And from the Bible, as ye sow, so shall ye reap. It was mostly jargon from the streets, yet it held basic truths. Do your thing and everything will follow.

I was in Odyssey House for six months, and then there was an upheaval. The clinical director, a psychiatrist, fired the director and the assistant director, both ex-addicts. A lot of us felt that they were really the people that we were there for. So we all left, about twenty-three people. We slept on the floor of my friend's grandmother's living room for a week. I had just had a hernia operation and I had a Blue Cross check. We cashed it and lived off the money. I was not going to do drugs again.

We went to a place upstate, a retreat that a church gave us, and we stayed there for a couple of months. Then we negotiated with Phoenix House, and the whole group was accepted there.

I made one big mistake. Shortly after I entered Phoenix House, I left to go to visit my girlfriend. Phoenix House had a very strict rule: no contact with anyone on the outside for at least six or eight months. The visit to my girlfriend was a disaster, and I knew it. I knew I couldn't handle it. I was so emotionally uptight that I knew I couldn't stay out in the street. I went back to Phoenix House, but they wouldn't take me in. They made me go through their whole induction process again. It took me ten days to get back in and I asked my family to put me up in a hotel for those days. I didn't drink and I did not use any drugs for those ten days. I was that motivated to get back into the program, which I did. I started at the bottom again, worked my way up and had that same sense of being able to help a newer member who hadn't yet put heroin that far behind him.

In 1968, I went to work for Phoenix House. I went from resident to a staff member, until I decided I wanted to go back out into the world again. I was the first guy to ever leave Phoenix House legally, with a job and with his own apartment. I got a job as a stock clerk, ten hours a day,